Y0-DAD-574

DISCOVERING OUR
MAGNETIC SPEAKER WITHIN

DISCOVERING OUR MAGNETIC SPEAKER WITHIN

Tina Bakehouse

MANUSCRIPTS
PRESS

COPYRIGHT © 2023 TINA BAKEHOUSE
All rights reserved.

DISCOVERING OUR MAGNETIC SPEAKER WITHIN

ISBN
979-8-88926-768-3 *Paperback*
979-8-88926-769-0 *Ebook*
979-8-88926-510-8 *Hardcover*

To Jon, my son, Mom and Dad for your continued love, support, and compassionate listening ear as I worked through the wave of emotions while composing this book. And, especially to Stephanie Albright who always knew I'd write a book.

CONTENTS

————

INTRODUCTION

———

*The only person you are destined to become
is the person you decide to be.*

—RALPH WALDO EMERSON

Seated in the speech pathologist's dark, windowless basement office, the doctor shifts in her black, linen chair, gives a long sigh, takes off her dark glasses and says, "You have vocal cord nodules."

After two months of intense vocal therapy, my speech pathologist refers me to a surgeon who specializes in laryngology. After examination and analysis of my throat, he rubs his chin and declares, "You have two choices: have surgery and most likely your vocal pitch will lower, or it's possible nothing happens, and the damage is done, or six weeks of silence. No talking. No laughing. No cheating."

No talking?

No laughing?

No cheating, as in, *say nothing.*

Immediately, I think, "How can I communicate? Connect with others, for that's what I do. *That's who I am.*" Clearly, this doctor doesn't comprehend how much I love communicating with others and love laughing even more. I select the cheapest and hardest choice: six weeks of silence. Little do I know how difficult it will be.

During this time, I sit with myself. Analyzing my thoughts and notepad in hand, I listen to people's personal stories, jotting question after question on paper. I become richly curious and learn what people want more than anything is to share their story. To be seen. To be heard. To connect with others.

My six weeks of silence makes the abstract concept of "magnetic" more concrete. Magnetic communicators listen to the self and to others. Being "magnetic" attracts others to their message with their voice, body, energy, and overall essence. To relate with others requires first connecting with our authentic self.

Everyone can be a magnetic communicator.

If you can speak, you can be magnetic. Magnetic speaking involves a process. It's a commitment and choice. It takes time and hard work. *You're taking the first step by picking up this book.* This book will get you there without six weeks of silence. Although, there's value in doing that anyway.

In this book, I'll address three areas:

First, *magnetic speakers are aware of their mindset*: who we are and what we think affects what we say and do. I reflect on the following questions:

Who am I?

Am I being authentic?

What is my communication style?

Second, *magnetic speakers create clear messages*. Leaders identify their topic, organize ideas, and stay audience-centered in each context.

A farmer who's passionate about soil health wonders why no one inquires about his different farming practices. I ask him, "Are you talking about it?" When he says, "no," I emphasize his need to be intentional, simple, clear, and willing to share his message. "Speeches require you to simplify. The average adult reads 300 words per minute, but people can only follow speech closely at around 150-160 words per minute" (Coleman 2014). Oral communication varies from written communication because it's ephemeral, repetitive, and more conversational, which adds to the challenge of consistently crafting an engaging message.

Third, *magnetic speakers express appropriate mechanics with their voice and body to create powerful presence and desired impact.*

Public speaking is a real fear. Almost eighty out of one hundred people experience public speaking anxiety at a small or large scale (Raja 2017). Additionally, in a study, 75 percent of college students admit they fear public speaking, yet 95 percent agree with proper counseling, instruction, and coaching, they can overcome the fear (Raja 2017). While speaking ranks as a common fear, most psychologists view it as an irrational fear one can easily overcome. The question becomes, why aren't anxious speakers seeking professional support to improve their skills?

Speaking consultant Carmine Gallo highlights 70 percent of employed Americans agree effective communication is critical to success at work (2014). A study explores the help-seeking behavior and finds gender as the most significant factor in determining the intention and effort for improving the skill of communication (Nelson, Whitfield, and Moreau 2012). Women were more likely to ask for help, while men were less likely. Researchers evaluated some perceive seeking help as a potential risk, diminishing their sense of power. Finally, both genders were less likely to seek help based on perception of costs. The strongest and most successful leaders communicate effectively. They invest in coaching and request feedback to continue to grow this skill. Yet, even though most people are aware lacking effective communication skills has a negative impact on their career, several still fail to remedy this deficiency.

WHAT PREVENTS LEADERS FROM BEING MORE MAGNETIC?

All of us can run on autopilot. We wake each morning. Talk on the phone to family and friends. Talk to our boss and team. We're talking, yet not being intentional with our ideas and message. Thus, we fail to be *magnetic* by not connecting with ourselves or others.

Leaders work constantly and fail to make time to prepare and speak their passion. Nancy Duarte, speaker and communication trainer, recommends spending thirty hours for each hour you speak, which doesn't include visual aids and practice (Duarte 2023). In addition to the necessary time commitment, 90 percent of speaking anxiety comes from lack of preparation (Zauderer 2023). Whether you're unsure how to create a message, fear presenting in front of an audience, or fail to make the time, it's vital to invest in discovering your speaker style.

After a year of intense vocal therapy and rest, a mindset and job change, my voice appears. My lower vocal pitch and breathy quality emphasize the need for rest and presence. This entails listening to my body, voice, and others when they speak. As a communication consultant and coach, leader, nature-lover, spouse, and mom, losing my voice opens my eyes to what's possible.

Fast forward years later, and I must find my voice again.

March 16, 2020, marks the start of the US pandemic. Suddenly, I'm homeschooling my fourth grade son and 85 percent of my professional bank job vanishes, not to mention the absence of speaking engagements, networking, and socializing off the farm. For more than a year, I feel disconnected. Eventually, my ten-year passion project evolves into a full-time communication consulting business: Tina B. LLC.

While marketing my business online, for the first time, I discover what my clients feel—insecurity, analysis paralysis, even crippled with perfectionism. Self-doubting thoughts pop in my head: Will my technology work? Do I look good enough on camera? Will people listen to me?

Am I magnetic?

HOW CAN WE *BE* A MAGNETIC SPEAKER?

This book explores my journey, what I've learned, and provides stories and strategies from experts for how leaders can be more magnetic on any stage. Practical exercises and reflection questions are included at the end of each chapter to support you to have a more magnetic mind, message, and mechanics.

As a CEO, nonprofit executive director, manager, service-based coach, or business owner, this book guides you to show up as the "who that you are." Whether you're communicating formally on a stage, leading a team meeting, sharing a new idea, or having a conversation with a potential client, all entail tuning inward to your authentic speaker style. The ideas framed in this book strengthen you to reach your full, magnetic potential.

How do you get there? What does it look like? Feel like?

Your success, influence, and overall impact are determined by expressing self-love and awareness, audience-centeredness, a willingness to get curious with message-meaning, and co-creating with others for the greater good. We need to embrace who we are and have the courage to understand more about communication styles and preferences. We must be okay with differences and presenting uncomfortable conversations or big ideas. Growth, true expansion, is leaning into the uncomfortable and getting good with uncertainty. How we show up in a space, use our words, and see each other, moves the conversation forward.

This book is for the people who to want to become more aware of their speaker style and be magnetic communicators. As leaders and advocates for change, we must guide our voice with our hearts and not settle for less than doing our best, a personal agreement (Ruiz 1997, 75). How can you be and communicate your best?

I, like others, for years, discover my life is on autopilot. We wake up each day and go through the motions. Losing my voice forced me to really stop. To pause. To think. We are called "human beings," not "human doers." Our purpose is to create. To speak. To be who we are. Let go of the doing and be in our being. Share what's in our hearts with magnetism to design the desired impact.

Through the course of this book, I'll discuss:

Who am I, and why does self-awareness matter?

What are strategies for creating an engaging message?

How do we strengthen our vocal and physical presence to connect with audiences?

Become inspired by experts and clients' insights and stories. Stories teach us what it means to be human, to grow, to move forward, and change. If you believe you're a magnetic speaker, put in the work, and do the reps, you can become one. You have the desire, now, let's put that desire into action. I hope you'll use this book as a reference guide. Write in it and respond to the reflection questions. Reflection leads to growth and change.

You can learn from others to stretch and lean into your essence, your sense of being. When you communicate, be you, the real you. When you do, others notice and connect.

True magnetism comes from within.

PART I

YOUR MAGNETIC MIND

WHAT DOES IT MEAN TO BE A MAGNETIC SPEAKER?

Speech is power: Speech is to persuade, to convert, to compel.

—RALPH WALDO EMERSON

After a long day at school, my son Rory comes home and hands me a ticket for an evening speaking event. Earlier at an assembly, keynote speaker and teen advocate Terrence Lee Talley addresses my son's junior/senior high school. His presentation "Never Give Up" focuses on letting go of anger and finding inner peace.

Initially, I resist. I have a meeting with a client at the same time. Yet, in the face of my son's passionate persistence, I can't say "no," especially when he says, "Mom. I want to know if this speaker is what you call 'magnetic.' Does he need your coaching?"

I'm hooked.

The emcee introduces the speaker. Expressing a big, earnest, toothy smile, presenter Talley bounces up the aisle bordered with shouting teenagers. Rory's desperation for me to attend, along with his curiosity about the speaker's magnetism, pique my interest. I decide to analyze this speaker's content and delivery and pose this question to answer:

What makes a speaker magnetic?

> *Dress for your audience.* Talley wears jeans, a t-shirt, and high-top tennis shoes, an approachable and relevant style for teens.

> *Build rapport and encourage audience participation.* The speaker requests audience stories to prompt immediate feedback.

> *Share personal and emotional stories to illustrate a point.* "A mother ceases to hug, kiss, or say, 'I love you' because she claims her thirteen-year-old daughter is no longer a baby," says Talley. He continues, "The daughter wipes her face with her mother's lipstick-printed tissue for affection." This story emphasizes everyone needs and deserves love at any age.

> *Express emotions and your personal transformation.* Talley communicates taking full responsibility for his anger and releases all animosity toward his dad. His honesty and compassion evoke emotion.

In a survey, following the talk, twenty-two high school students describe him as "motivational, inspiring, and impactful."

Deliver naturally. Rory says, "Talley showed excitement when the story went well and spoke softly when the story was sad." Throughout the presentation, Talley raises the corners of his mouth and arches his eyebrows enthusiastically, projects intense and powerful vocal inflection, steps downstage, leans forward, and gestures his full palms for emphasis to connect with his audience.

At the end of the speech, Talley asks the audience, "Who's ready to be free?" My son, a reserved observer, walks to the front of the stage to join other teens moved by his message. Talley does more than inspire; his persuasive appeal motivates my son and others to act.

MAGNETIC SPEAKER DEFINED

During a science unit, my third grade teacher Mrs. Carlisle demonstrates how magnets work. Fascinated, I observe two iron elements sticking together. She illuminates this phenomenon: two objects attract and attach because iron, nickel, or cobalt contain certain bonding components. She explains rocks or wood cannot conduct the same electric field as iron or nickel. I observe science and experience magnetism. Great teachers show, draw you in, and make a long-lasting impact, same as strong speakers.

Curious about the meaning of "magnetic" in the context of communication, I speak with others in the field. Erik Dominguez, communication consultant, says, "We struggle to define 'magnetic speaker,' yet we know it when we see it. Magnetic speaking is hard to quantify, for it's like asking what makes a professional athlete or musician professional. There's both a science and art to guide the speaker, for they should be authentic, have integrity, and make a lasting impact." Psychotherapist, writer/performer Jude Treder-Wolff says, "Being magnetic with your presentation is a combination of being educated, enlightened, having clarity on a point, being disciplined with the message, and combining that with heart and authenticity." From my experience and research, I define "magnetic speaker" as someone who's emotionally connected and intellectually charged to attract their audience with their words, voice, body, energy, and overall essence to achieve a desired impact and outcome.

To be magnetic, engage and connect others to your authentic, charismatic approach, the individual you.

In this chapter, I use the word "charismatic" synonymously with "magnetic." Rooted in feelings and values, the *Oxford Reference* defines charisma as a "quality possessed by some individuals that encourages others to listen and follow" (2023). The term "attractiveness" means appealing, drawing audience members in, and motivating them to listen. While being attractive helps on a first date, it's the speaker's ability to connect with their energy rather than their dashing looks. Charisma, like magnetism, exerts an attractive force.

Organizational Professor John Antonakis's TEDx Talk stresses communicating with charisma requires three elements:

1. Frame ideas to paint a picture and focus attention with metaphor and stories, contrasts, rhetorical questions, lists, and repetitions

2. Provide justification through moral conviction, sentiments, ambitious goals, and confidence

3. Deliver in an animated and passionate way with voice, gestures, and other tactics (Antonakis 2015).

Magnetic speakers modify their style based on the speaking context and audience's expectations, using their voice, body, energy, and message. Therefore, magnetic speakers balance Aristotle's logos, ethos, and pathos. They have authority on the topic, establish authentic integrity, and show emotion through a personalized, persuasive delivery style.

It all starts with an idea.

Magnetic communication starts with the openness to share ideas and craft intentional content. In her TEDxEast Talk, speaking trainer Nancy Duarte clarifies every powerful presentation contains two factors: "What is and what could be" (Duarte 2012). Furthermore, she suggests, "an idea stays powerless if it stays inside of you… and [presentations] have the power to change the world" (Duarte 2012). For example, Nelson Mandela spoke of freedom and democracy and demonstrated peace in prison. John F. Kennedy persuaded Americans to take on a space challenge. Hilary Clinton made history in 2016 as the first woman to run for President of the United States. Magnetism moves forward concepts and generates powerful influences in the world.

MAGNETIC SPEAKING ATTRIBUTES

Magnetism comes from connecting to the self and others. There is a myriad of ways to engage, stay engaged, and bond with your audience. International speaker and presentation trainer Brian Drury discusses how a speaker exemplifies magnetism in an interview. Drury says, "Magnetic speaking is having a genuine belief in what you talk about and meets the following qualifications: Confidence in the subject matter; confidence in presentation skills; and an understanding that they [the speaker] are there for the audience and not for themselves."

Drury describes his years of deep study in psychology and human behavior, specifically with his speaking mentor Sean Stephenson. We both believe magnetic speakers value having a clear, attentive concentration and understanding that they are speaking for a specific audience. The speaker's "why" needs to focus on providing a fresh perspective and attracting their audience to listen and think. Drury emphasizes high-performing, successful speakers approach each speech with an attitude to serve and must understand how their audience's minds work to create shifts in thinking and behavior. This evolution entails the speaker to explore brain functionality and exhibit clear self-awareness.

My Personal Recommendation for Being Magnetic

> Personify self-love and self-awareness. Embody
> your idiosyncrasies in word choices, vocal delivery,

and body language to meet the needs of the speaking context.

Believe and trust in the self and message. Inner belief shows in your content and delivery.

Express passionately charged energy from within. Like a candle's flame glows brightly, hot to the touch, speakers shine their light of ideas when they speak.

Attract others to listen with style.

Connect with the self and others. Communication is a shared experience, an ongoing sending and receiving of messages.

How do you become a more magnetic speaker in any given situation?

Look the part. Feel your message. Start with what your audience knows. Use stories to connect and share life lessons. Trust yourself.

To be magnetic, compose clear, passionate messages to land in the hearts of others.

CAN ANYONE BE A MAGNETIC SPEAKER?

The idea of "magnetism" translates as a descriptor for how we communicate. Magnets connect with one another like human beings magnetize other humans with speech, not only formally on stage but also in boardroom discussions, team meetings, or with current or prospective clients. How do communicators engage an audience and maintain their attention? Does everyone have this ability regardless of personality?

In one word: *yes.*

As humans, we label and categorize. For example, we may say, "You're funny" or "You're smart." What makes a person "funny" or "smart?" Similarly, we have opinions for the word "magnetic." When you think of a "magnetic" person, who do you picture? A loud, booming voice, animated facial expressions, large gestures, and expressive body? A high-energy and passionate Oprah type? Oprah engages audiences with strong, enchanting performances, yet her sense of belonging to who she is and connection to the audience's needs and passion for her topic attract audience attention. Contrast her style with NPR interviewer Terry Gross's calm, inquisitive method, thoughtful questions, and active listening to appeal audiences to her show. Their words, energy, and style captivate and solicit attention.

Quieter types can be magnetic.

Culturally, introversion has been associated with being quiet and dull and can push introverts to be inauthentic when speaking or choose not to speak at all. Some of my introverted friends have vocalized they internalize the pressure to be vocally and physically loud when speaking. It's possible extroverts dominate and communicate their inner thoughts aloud continuously and gain more energy. This tires introverts. My introverted spouse Lyle says, "I don't want to fight to get a word in. It's just too much work." The most engaging speakers possess a deliberative and powerful presence. Gandhi's strong silence and peaceful demeanor demanded massive responses for social justice. Charisma connects you to the audience, not how loud you are. The Dalai Lama is as magnetic as Tony Robbins, just in a different way.

Being a charismatic speaker requires you to be who you are, the very essence of you.

Researcher, storyteller, and author Brené Brown is one of my favorite speakers. Brown, known for her authenticity, has said, "To be authentic, we must cultivate the courage to be imperfect—and vulnerable. We have to believe that we are fundamentally worthy of love and acceptance, just as we are. I've learned that there is no better way to invite more grace, gratitude, and joy into our lives than by mindfully practicing authenticity" (Brown 2014). Brown doesn't read her speeches. Instead, she engages in a conversation with the audience and exposes her imperfection and expresses vulnerability as she navigates the challenges of being a wife, mom, and shame researcher.

Speech-givers differentiate from magnetic speakers: speech-givers read a script without emotion and lack care for their audience. Conversely, magnetic speakers analyze the circumstance and align their content to the context. Director of TED speaker coaching Briar Goldberg says, "The next time you're preparing to speak to a group, remember to keep your audience at the center of your communication. One way to do this is to ask yourself: What gift are you giving to your audience" (Goldberg 2019)? Instead of giving a speech, be a communicator. Your audience will appreciate the gift.

Whether you're more energized and loud or quite the opposite, all styles have a means to magnetism. Explore your authentic speaker style. Be with your audience. Co-create messages, open to the dance of conversation. No matter your skill in speaking, you can reach your fullest potential. Practice makes permanent.

MAGNETISM CAN BE LEARNED

While being magnetic comes more naturally for some speakers, the ability to possess more charisma in your communication style is possible. Speakers connect, compare, and contrast with their words, voice, and body (Antonakis, Fenley, and Liechti 2012, 127-130). Researchers describe these elements as "charismatic leadership tactics." They define charisma as rooting in a balance of Aristotle's logos, ethos, and pathos. If a speaker balances authority, integrity, and emotion, the audience feels it. The authors list the following twelve teachable leadership traits to a more charismatic speaking style:

"*Verbal Tactics*:
Metaphors, similes, and analogies
Stories and anecdotes
Contrasts
Rhetorical questions
Expressions of moral conviction
Reflections of the group's sentiments
Three-part lists
The setting of high goals
Conveying confidence

Nonverbal Tactics:
Animated voice
Facial expressions
Gestures"

(ANTONAKIS, FENLEY,
AND LIECHTI 2012, 127-130).

Andrew Tarvin, humor engineer and CEO of Humor That Works, describes magnetism is an attraction, pulling people in. This skill can be learned, for it's not something you're born with or part of a genetic code. He discusses, like humor, magnetism comes through practice and repetition. It necessitates locating safe spaces for this practice. Tarvin emphasizes magnetism requires being intentional and learning from audience feedback; translation: no engagement, no magnetism.

Why does being charismatic matter?

Researchers discover people who practice charismatic traits improve leadership style and competency ratings from others by 60 percent (Antonakis, Fenley, and Liechti 2012, 127-130). If your team senses your inner strength and passionate energy, they'll perceive you in a more positive way and are more apt to respond to the energy they're feeling from you. Magnetic speaking comes from the heart and balances with the knowledge of the mind. Confident mindset, energy, and strategy are what best reach your audience.

Magnetism takes strategy and effort.

**TO BE A MAGNETIC SPEAKER, THIS BOOK
ADDRESSES THE FOLLOWING:**

Mind
Personality
Mindset
Communication Style

Message
Passion
Creative Style
Flow

Mechanics
Vocal and Physical Delivery
Forgiveness
Practice

Audience-centeredness—it's about them… always.

Theatre professor Gretta Berghammer advises, "A magnetic speaker owns their knowledge; they've lived it, applied it, tested it, improved on it, shared it, and learn by the doing." This book will support your magnetic speaker journey. I've lived it, applied it, tested it, and want to share it with you, to have you learn by doing, to be the magnetic speaker you are meant to be.

EXERCISE

Listen and watch a TED talk presentation online. Take note of what elements draw you to listen. How do speaker's word choices attract you to the message? What vocal and physical delivery choices intrigue you? What proves to be distracting? What would you do differently to make the presentation more magnetic?

REFLECTION QUESTIONS

What does "magnetic speaker" mean to me?

What does being "magnetic" feel like?

Do I see myself as a "magnetic speaker?"

What steps can I take to increase my magnetism?

What can I do now to practice being magnetic?

THE WHO THAT WE ARE: OUR SOULS SPEAK

——

Be yourself. The worst talks are the ones where someone
is trying to be someone they aren't. If you're generally
goofy, be goofy. If you are emotional, then be emotional.

—SALMAN KHAN, ACTOR, FILM PRODUCER

"Tina Mae Kneisel was born November 28, 1975, at Cass
County Memorial Hospital in Atlantic, Iowa to two proud
parents." I scan the faded, type-written pages of my eighth
grade autobiography. As the quintessential 1980s over-permed,
metal mouth, goggle-glasses and stone-washed, Jordache
jeans-wearing junior high kid, I delve into my paper and
read categories of what's important to me: family and friends,
personal interests, skills, values, and dreams. I read further. I
don't know what surprises me more, the fact I still love roller
skating at middle age, or I'm old enough to have composed
a paper on an old-school typewriter, or I explore the deeper
parts of myself that make me me at thirteen years old.

As I've reached middle age, I've investigated the great search of knowing who I am. I love the television series *Mister Rogers' Neighborhood* for the great imagination and Land of Make Believe and Fred Rogers' mantra, "I like you just the way you are." His beautiful sentiment inspires youngsters to accept themselves as is. This external encouragement can lead us to value other people's opinions more than our own.

Self-concept impacts communication. *The American Psychology Dictionary* defines self-concept as "one's description and evaluation of oneself, including psychological and physical characteristics, qualities, skills, and roles" (2023). Magnetic communication derives from self-awareness of these traits, from the inner knowing of who we are, embracing our vulnerability, being authentic and true, and speaking from the heart.

Magnetism requires self-awareness.

DEFINING AND UNDERSTANDING THE SELF

Social psychologist Amy Cuddy highlights how multifaceted and complex the self is (2015, 43). The self is expressed through thoughts, feelings, values, and behaviors. We live by certain mental scripts each day. The story we think and tell ourselves becomes our reality. Thoughts become perception, and perception becomes how we behave and communicate with others. As our mind's architect, we train our brain to either communicate negatively or effectively and powerfully dynamic as the authentic self. Cuddy states, "Sometimes you have to get out of the way of yourself to be yourself" (2015, 28). Additionally, she cites organizational behavior professor Laura Morgan Roberts' four core questions to answer, "Who am I?":

"What three words best describe you? What kind of presence do you desire?

What is unique about you that leads to your best performance? What energy do you share?

When was there a moment (at work or home) that something felt 'right' or 'natural?' How can you duplicate that feeling and behave in a certain way?

What are your signature strengths, and how can you use them for public speaking"

(CUDDY 2015, 46)?

Additionally, master coach Maria Nemeth, PhD, breaks down the self into layers, from pretending to fearing our real self to then identifying who we really are. To know the self, explore and be aware of these layers (2023).

Researchers define self-awareness as "the ability to see oneself as separate from others" (Powell, Honey, and Symbaluk 2017, 343), and "the extent to which people are consciously aware of their internal states and their interactions or relationships with others" (Sutton 2016, 443). During my undergraduate communication studies work, I learn about Joseph Luft and Harry Ingham's Johari Window Model. This model analyzes four levels of self-awareness: what we and others both know; what we know and others don't know about ourselves; what others know and we don't; and what is unknown to both the self and others. During my early twenties, I grasp the complexity of the self and how others can have different perceptions of me.

Psychologist Tasha Eurich classifies two types of self-awareness: "*internal self-awareness*, represents how clearly we see our own values, passions, aspirations, fit with our environment, reactions (including thoughts, feelings, behaviors, strengths, and weaknesses), and impact on others. The second category, *external self-awareness*, means understanding how other people view us, in terms of those same factors listed above" (2018). Surprisingly, Eurich concludes from research most people believe they're self-aware, yet only 10-15 percent are (2018).

Clarifying the unknown of the self transpires from understanding our cognitive behavior—how we think, learn, and perceive the world—and our experiences with others. Both directly influence what we say and do. Our mental representation of the world varies from person to person because our brain structure, function, processing speed, and memory vary (Anderson 2020, 392). Researchers state our brain sends us information based on previous experiences and architects our nervous system (Kolb, Whishaw, and Teskey 2019, 64-65). Thus, brain variation impacts what information we select and conceptualize, which affects communication patterns.

Individualized use and style of language and symbols influence audience connection. For example, a speaker who grew up in Texas or another southern state may use the term "y'all" to relate intimately to their audience. Contrast the previous style with animal welfare advocate Temple Grandin, who's autistic and thinks in pictures. She may express her ideas candidly, with visual precision in a non-linear way.

Self-aware speakers monitor, manage their cognition, and track and adapt their communication and behavior to meet the needs of their audience. They assess the need for changes to affect the impact. We develop personal rules to include what we think and tell ourselves, which influence our behavior (Powell, Honey, and Symbaluk 2017). A speaker may establish a rule to say aloud positive affirmations prior to each communicative event because they believe this act influences their success.

Recently, I visited a friend, theatre educator Sonia, to celebrate earning her master's to become a licensed mental health therapist. I ask Sonia, "Why is it important to be self-aware?"

She says, "There's value in knowing yourself to communicate effectively. I was diagnosed with ADHD later in life. That, coupled with trauma, can heighten the symptoms of ADHD, which affects my communication patterns. I'm aware words just come flying out of my mouth. My communication style tends to be really direct and blunt. Super honest and transparent. For people who adhere or subscribe to having social graces, or it's all about politeness, that's not how I operate, which can come off abrasive or aggressive, or too much. I understand I have a big personality. So, knowing that, I'll say, 'I'm neurodivergent (differing in mental function),' usually in an entertaining way, but it can possibly exhaust you. I give this warning label or disclaimer because I'd never want to upset or harm another person because of the way I talk."

Sonia is unapologetic for being herself and values her ability to be "super transparent and honest." As a mindful communicator who's aware her brain functions differently, she requests feedback to ensure others are comfortable. Thus, Sonia's self-awareness allows her to adapt her communication style, so others receive her message effectively.

Knowing yourself serves as a tool for your toolbox to reach common understanding and effectively deliver a clearer message.

WHAT WE THINK IS WHO WE ARE

Defining and feeling who we are influences our message. You've heard the phrase, "mind over matter." If a speaker thinks and believes the statement, "I am confident," then their body and words mirror this remark. If, however, a speaker perceives no one cares for them or their message, their body language may exhibit a slouched, closed, or tight style, and their voice may sound stiff or shaky. What you think and say is who you become.

My spouse knows who he is. Lyle doesn't add superfluous words or justification. He works, communicates, and lives daily in a grounded state of being. As a speaker, he's calm and deliberate, with an unwavering desire to speak about soil health. Lyle's singular, passionate soil health message influences audiences to understand their choices all depend on the soil. He is who he is: undeniably and without question.

Author Deepak Chopra explains stillness allows our essence to shine through (1994). Chopra notes our full potential insists on acknowledging we're infinitely creative, invincible, simplistic, and full of bliss when we practice nonjudgment of the self. Ignoring outer world influences leads to the pureness of our potential. When we're fully present and grounded in a neutral state, we avoid needing validation from others. We release the need to control situations and people. Instead, stand in the confident "I am" state. If we remove the opinions of others, we experience freedom and self-love.

Real power comes from within.

The ego feeds on control, taps into fear, and cares about others' approval. Psychologist Sigmund Freud defines ego as "what the person is aware of when they think about themselves and is what they usually try to project toward others [...] It is the decision-making component of personality" (McLeod 2023). Our egos can control us or not. Magnetic speakers admonish the ego's voice and fear-based feelings and responses.

In an online conversation with friend and life coach Stacey, she centers on "enoughness." She discloses her experience of creating her business, the difficulty of marketing, the amount of visibility it takes, and how vulnerable she feels. She expresses the challenge of self-love and valuing all of herself inside and out. We discuss how we feel in the inside makes itself known on the outside. Stacey encourages me to place Post-its on my computer that say: "My body is valuable. My face is valuable. My voice is valuable. I am valuable. I am enough." These visual images remind me to be present, calm, and confident during each virtual conversation and presentation.

To speak and connect, be open to possibilities, then appreciate and achieve your pure potential.

WHAT'S YOUR UNDERLYING BELIEF ABOUT YOURSELF AS A SPEAKER?

Starting my business, I struggle. I don't know what I'm doing. During an online networking event, attendees present a one- to two-minute speech about themselves and their business. I spew a large list, including my passion for speaking, story-telling, and farm. One stern man glares and says sharply, "I'm confused. You need to work on your pitch. You should hire me to help you. You don't know who you are or what you're doing." His terse voice stings me deeply. While his piercing tone and words hurt, my self-doubt propels into insecure energy and an anxious speaking style. I race through words, grasp for breath, and slump my posture. My lack of confidence influences my content and hurts my impact. This results in zero follow-up networking calls.

You create the state of your mind. Dr. Joseph Murphy's work concentrates on the subconscious mind, the decision-making part of the brain that works without our awareness (McMahan 2019). Murphy stresses we are what we think all day. He emphasizes our subconscious mind's ability to be open to suggestions, create positive and passionate thoughts, and the use of visualization to release negative blocks and replace fear. He declares we can take charge of our thoughts. We can plant seeds of desire in the garden of our mind.

Deepak Chopra highlights what we focus on, our words, thoughts, and deeds are a thread that returns (2010, 53-55). Negative thoughts, motivated attention, and vocalizing harsh words heighten energy. Beliefs initiate; we act more like what we say and think. Others either gravitate toward our energy or are repelled by it as I experienced in the past networking event.

My clients have said, "I can't do Facebook Lives. I ramble and talk too much." This absolute "can't" and proclamation, "I talk too much" represents the individual's perception of their ability. Negative thoughts and energy translate in the body. Think. Feel. Act.

Magnetic speakers dig deeper. They explore and examine the harder questions.

What's my true nature? How do I express myself with integrity?

Musician, author, and podcaster Andy Mort expounds on the importance of magnetic energy. He says, "It's feeling a oneness with the audience, hanging on the same page." Through self-exploration, he has grown to define himself as a "gentle rebel," which means firm backing, a soft front, holding one's position, true acceptance, fully creative, seeing the human.

His podcast and client conversations focus on "gentleness." After he analyzes past podcasts, Mort notices a different energy. He says, "I noticed how I've changed my tone, vocal delivery, a lot. There was a harshness, holding tightly, intensity. I wasn't listening to the interviewees. I was thinking during the interview: 'How can I make this work?' I went from massively preparing to trusting instead, flowing into the conversation. Preparation helped me touch on certain points." Mort shifts to his true self. Thus, he experiences a freeing, real energy, being in his being, and getting okay with awkward silence, where true connection can be found.

Feelings are fleeting. We mirror the other, and they mirror us. Ask yourself, "What energy do I want to share with this audience? What energy do I want to leave in the space?" Your words generate long-lasting impacts; therefore, it's essential for your heart to guide your thoughts and words. Surrender and soften your effort. During a coaching session, Stephanie Albright, intuitive and spiritual guide, asks me, "Why are you trying so hard?" To "try" means you're failing to "be," morphing into someone else.

Magnetic speakers don't try. They "be."

THE BENEFITS OF BEING SELF-AWARE

Self-awareness empowers the speaker and impacts change.

In a conversation, author Michael Marvosh talks about the importance of speaking and living with integrity, your true principles, consistently to empower the self. He examines the possibility of changing our minds for greatness. Marvosh expresses, "Whatever power we want to create in the world must necessarily come from the authentic self. If we're showing up as we think other people would have us be, the power we have in that space is, at best, borrowed from those people. If we're more true to self, the more power we have." Magnetic connections happen when speakers come ready, fully focused on love of the self, audience, and topic instead of worrying about potential judgments. My past clients have witnessed growth in their businesses, deeper connections with teams and clients, and legislation policy exposure and change based on their powerful speech.

Self-awareness improves communication skills and relationships.

Researchers conduct a study with undergraduate nursing students, which involves assessing nurses' care for patients with their self-awareness (Li et al. 2022). They find a significant positive correlation between undergraduate nursing students' caring ability and their self-awareness to improved communication proficiency. They conclude educators can guide and cultivate self-awareness and communication skills to foster improved clinical relationships. For example, when someone says a vague phrase, "Hey, grab that. It's over there," and assumes the listener knows what "that" and "there" are, they hurt the overall connection with the person. Instead, if we articulate our care for the other, clarify the words we use, and check for understanding, we strengthen our interpersonal relationships.

Self-awareness leads to desired impact and results.

Keynote speaker and certified professional coach Ivy Woolf Turk illustrates the importance of self-awareness to communicate more effectively. A year prior, Turk hires a storytelling coach to assist in understanding herself. The coach pushes her to do the inner work of identifying key stories from her last ten years of life. Turk learns her stories follow three patterns: 1) she knows how to ask for help; 2) she doesn't stay stuck ruminating but takes action; and 3) she's much stronger than she believes.

Pausing to listen to her feelings around a pivotal moment, identifying any limiting beliefs, and then creating a three-point plan, support Turk to craft messages to resonate with her and the audience. She presents a speech to businesswomen at a chamber of commerce event. Turk thinks about who the audience is and sets an intention for the speech: to be vulnerable (know, like, and trust), to inspire using her authentic story, and to gain new clients. "I assessed my way of communicating, for use of language and energy matters," says Turk. What was the result following her talk? A long line of interested clients desiring to work with her. Turk emphasizes, "Had I not harmonized my inner and outer world of Ivy, my talk wouldn't have landed so powerfully." From her inner work, knowing who she is through the powerful tool of storytelling, Turk presents magnetically, stands in her knowing, and achieves her desired outcome.

However, knowing the true self poses challenges. Holistic Naturopath Dr. Caryn Willens explains, "We all have a part of us we're hiding. Women in particular feel shame. While our experiences are different, we're all alike. When we accept it's not us, it's our childhood, we can stop hiding." Magnetic speakers let go of past stories, release power from what they've learned that doesn't serve them, and open intuitively to respond from the heart.

DO THE INNER WORK TO BE THE SELF

Others affect our energy. Energy influences a reaction. To work through negative thoughts, speaker and author Byron Katie has developed "the work." Presenters of "The Work," Thom Herman and Lee Greenbaum describe it as a powerful program evoking in the method of self-inquiry (Katie 2023).

The Process of Byron Katie's The Work:

Step 1: Notice—Who or what upsets you? Why? Notice, name the situation, and feel the emotion.

Step 2: Write—As an outside observer, judge the situation. Express without censorship the cause of your stress.

Step 3: Question—Select a specific statement or thought and question if it's true. Listen and wait for the response (Katie 2023).

Katie says, "I discovered that when I believed my thoughts, I suffered, but when I didn't believe them, I didn't suffer, and that this is true for every human being. Freedom is as simple as that" (2023). Our brains are capable of consistently constructing negative thoughts over and over again. These negative thoughts create patterns. The patterns influence communication style and behavior. Freeing the self from negative thoughts leads to magnetism. Ask yourself: Is what and how I am responding true to who I am? Who am I being in this situation? I've changed my thought from, "There are too many and much better communication consultants in the world than me," to "I am confident and unique and no one consults and coaches like me."

Creating your magnetic messages depends on self-aware-ness of your personality, past experiences, value system, and intentionality.

TINA'S TIPS TO BE THE SELF
Tune inward to your energy and know your purpose.

Energy remains a universal language. It's a powerful, author-itative force. In the fable, *The Alchemist*, author Paulo Coelho writes of Santiago who dreams and ventures on a long journey to follow his life purpose (1995). Through multiple conversations and experiences, Santiago discovers to strive to be his best and live his personal legend. Like Santiago, I've learned my purpose has evolved to motivate growth-oriented, heart-centered leaders who are urgent to craft powerful messages with confidence and clarity, so they can communicate their mission to the world and make a difference in a big way. I say this statement every day to focus my intention and energy to achieve this purpose.

Listen to your inner knowing. You embody more than your achievements and credentials. Ask: What am I thinking? Feeling? Dig deep inside. If you take the time to explore, the answers will be revealed within you. Being authentic and at peace with ourselves, communicating magnetically, requires self-love. By loving ourselves, feeling it, and knowing it, we show and express our love to others.

Release self-doubt.

Let go of self-doubt and the ego, the part of you who cares about the external world. The ego masks your identity, enforces hierarchies, isolates, and provides obstacles for growth. How do you speak to others about yourself? The dickcissel, a small, yellow-breasted midwestern bird, takes flight in prairie grasslands singing its own song freely in its being. You and your words can take flight. It's a choice. Will you embody your inner dickcissel, fly with a vibrant, centered-confidence, and speak your personal song? Label and face doubting thoughts. I wrote my doubts on paper, tore them into shreds, and said, "These doubts are gone."

Take time to space out and clear your brain.

Our brain invents, uses language, and expresses emotion. *Medical News Today* explains the notion we have one dominant side of the brain over the other is a myth (2020). In a study, researchers measure the activity of both hemispheres of the brain using an MRI scanner. The scan concludes people do not have a dominant side and use both hemispheres (Nielsen et al. 2013). Yet, we get stuck. Author Lisa Lenard-Cook explains our brains create and edit (2008, 4-8). To gain access to our creativity, engage the brain in nonverbal, non-analytic activities such as showering, jogging, or gardening.

Quiet your mind. Relax. Let go. Take a brief phrase and repeat it to stay centered in the self. Thinking converts energy. What activates or energizes you in a positive way? Pay close attention to your thoughts, behaviors, and let go of the future. Future thoughts generate anxiety. Past thoughts construct a depressive state of mind.

Change your words from "I feel" to "I know." Let your intuition guide you. See your greatness for what it is and who you are. Be a wild rose: cultivate ideas, grow your voice freely, open up, and present in your own beautiful way.

Embrace your uniqueness, fully untamed, unapologetically as yourself.

EXERCISES

How do you learn? What is your way of processing information? Journal about your cognitive way of being.

Make a list of past experiences. What are the stories attached to those memories? How will you write the story differently to be more magnetic?

Fill in the blanks:

I am...
I am...
I am...

From your responses, create a speaker vision statement. For example, "I am a passionate, connected, and confident speaker."

Post your vision statement in your office and car where you see it. Say it aloud each day. Own it. Feel it. Be it.

Explore who you are by taking an inventory of your choices. What do you read? Watch? How do you spend your time? These decisions influence your overall way of being.

REFLECTION QUESTIONS

Who am I?

What are my beliefs about myself?

How do I define myself as a speaker?

What are my beliefs about my speaking ability?

What stories have I told myself?

What's my new, magnetic story?

OWNING YOUR MAGNETIC PERSONALITY

If a man does not keep pace with his companions, perhaps it is because he hears a different drummer. Let him step to the music which he hears, however measured or far away.

—HENRY DAVID THOREAU

Starting my business, I'm terrified. Gripping stacks of freshly printed business cards, I walk into the loud networking space in hopes someone familiar will approach me. For the first time, I'm representing me and my business, not a university, nonprofit, or corporation, but me. This awareness paralyzes me. I think: Will anyone be interested in learning more? Will I attract new clients? *Will I be liked?*

These irrational questions whirl in my head, affecting my presence in the space. Instead of the fun, passionate, and confident leader, I suddenly feel pessimistic, worried, and lack self-trust. The negative, weighted thoughts translate into facial and body tension, larger gestures, and a boisterous, booming voice. My outer-self overcompensates for the inner anxiety of my mind.

Shortly thereafter, I venture to a horse ranch for a life-changing, guided coaching experience. My goal: let go of control and perfectionism. After observing the horse herd, I select to groom and become more acquainted with Dale, a stand-off-ish, isolated horse. Aware of his reticence, I wait. Staring into his dark, broad eyes, I build trust. Calmly and gently, I stroke his mane. Our bodies relax. One by one, the other four horses and Dale nuzzle my nose. Fully present, we engage in a dance and co-create a magical experience with our eyes, voices, and bodies.

During my time with Dale, I study my leadership and communication style. I admit to him how tough networking events are. How I want to connect at a deeper level than business elevator pitches. How I want to let go of the need to sell my business and perform. How I want to step back, communicate clearly with heart, and advocate for others. When present without an agenda, I stand in my power and truth.

Today, I've grown in knowledge and activated behavioral change. To lead, I emotionally regulate. To communicate, I let go of the mask. To connect, I find the "Dale" in the room, that reserved person who may be slower to connect with others, abstains from surface-level conversations, and desires in-depth connections. Effective leaders choose to be a present and active listener. To relate with others, they first connect with themselves. Moving forward, I navigate my thoughts and emotions and frame networking and speaking performances as heart-centered conversations. Entering spaces, I observe, listen, and refrain from the notion of "human doing" and embrace "human being."

Asking the wrong internal questions alters the state of mind and personality. Questions like, "How can I gain new clients? How can I be super-interesting and wicked smart? How do I get more positive attention?" Instead of being interested, I'm trying to be interesting. Instead of going with the intention to relate with others, I'm concerned about obtaining clients and growing my business. Instead of trusting myself, I change into an insecure, people-pleasing mode, trying too hard, burdened with heavy energy rather than joy.

Similarly, my client, financial advisor, Katie, speaks of the disconnection to herself every time she introduces her business at networking events. Following three months of my coaching program, a divorce attorney invites her to lunch. Katie says, "The attorney noticed my elevator pitch had changed. She didn't know I specialized with divorced women, and I wouldn't have changed my message had I not worked through it with you many times. I definitely displayed more confidence." Letting go of insecurity and getting intentional, Katie's words and overall presence emanated self-trust. Her dedicated and persevering personality radiated.

It's important to balance our inborn personality traits with the given circumstance. How does this transformation happen? What powers this change, so we can present ourselves in the most magnetic way and make the message noticeably more impactful? Instead of holding on to what isn't, embrace what is. Knowing our existing skills, behaviors, communication styles, and preferences helps us capitalize on current strengths rather than focus on weaknesses.

What holds you back from being more of who you are and communicate effectively?

Working with clients, I've found self-perception can limit performance. People categorize and label themselves and others with personality test results. Defining individuals from their scores influences communication, behavior, and overall connection. For example, the identification of "introvert" may have a negative connotation as someone who doesn't speak often or relate well with others instead of needing time alone for introspection. Perhaps the individual views the "introvert" classification as someone who doesn't enjoy communicating with people or thinking on their feet. These preconceived notions of the "negative assessment" can hold the introvert back from volunteering to speak and perform at their fullest potential. Inner thoughts may include, "I can't do this presentation" or "Someone else should lead the team." Instead, reflect and focus on strengths to prepare and present a powerful message.

Although knowing personality test results and communication preferences may hurt others and our self-perception, the outcomes can help speakers be more conscious of their natural inclinations. Psychology is vastly complex. Comprehending results from categorization systems like Myers-Briggs or CliftonStrengths organizes our thoughts, gives us words to define patterned ways of being, and provides useful strategies. Though they are imperfect, human-created tools, these instruments offer a starting place and means of language to pinpoint what's working or not effective with our communication style. Grasping the complexity of the self requires exploring the concept of personality through temperament and the Big Five Personality Traits.

DEFINING TEMPERAMENT

During a graduate course, Professor Dr. John McKenna draws an acorn on the board and invites students to respond to his question: "What would this acorn grow into if planted in fertile, Nebraska soil?" The class agrees an oak tree. He follows with the question: "What would an acorn become if planted in the arid climate and rocky soil of Colorado?" The answer: "An oak tree." This metaphor emphasizes the acorn's internal DNA, denoting temperament. While his example isn't scientifically perfect, it presents an appropriate analogy to contrast the concepts of nature (inborn) versus nurture (environment).

Temperament is not a new psychological concept. In the second century, Hippocrates defined the four, distinct types of bodily fluids, and later, the physician Galen established the four humors as melancholic, phlegmatic, sanguine, and choleric, which concentrate on the individual's emotional moods, defined behavioral patterns, and persistence of achieving desired goals (Keirsey 1998, 2-3). Social psychologist David Keirsey builds from this historical perspective and divides personality into temperament and character. Keirsey compares these two components to parts of a computer: *temperament* as our hardware, "a configuration of natural inclinations... a pre-disposition, our blood, our DNA" and *character* as our software, "the blending of our various habits, the environment, people you encounter, and experiences" (1998, 20).

Temperament = nature. Character = nurture.

The National Library of Medicine website defines temperament as "behavioral traits such as sociability (outgoing or shy), emotionality (easy-going or quick to react), activity level (high or low energy), attention level (focused or easily distracted), and persistence (determined or easily discouraged)" (2022). Furthermore, the website mentions genetics play a major role in behavior. In fact, "scientists estimate 20 to 60 percent of temperament is determined by genetics" (National Library of Medicine 2022). While this range is huge, it's important to note a portion of who we are is pre-determined by our genetic makeup, influencing our decision-making, communication and leadership style, and relatability with people.

UNDERSTANDING THE BIG FIVE PERSONALITY TRAITS

In his TEDx Talk, psychologist Brian Little clarifies how people have three natures: our biogenic nature (physiological), our sociogenic nature (culture), and our idiosyncratic nature (individuality) (2016). He highlights the Big Five Personality Traits gage success in life and articulates we're all smart in different ways.

Psychology expert Annabelle Lim provides definitions of the Big Five Traits:

"Conscientiousness—impulsive, disorganized versus disciplined, careful

Agreeableness—suspicious, uncooperative versus trusting, helpful

Neuroticism—calm, confident versus anxious, pessimistic

Openness to Experience—prefers routine, practical versus imaginative, spontaneous

Extroversion—reserved, thoughtful versus sociable, fun-loving"

(LIM 2023).

Scientists continue to debate the Big Five Traits' levels of hereditary and to what degree. A study assesses personality traits influence social outcomes, specifically active-empathetic listening and assertiveness (Sims 2016). Using self-reporting, this study investigates personality affects communication competence. Both agreeableness and openness predict higher levels of active listening, with extroversion as the biggest influence on the level of assertiveness. In an additional study, researchers find consistent hereditary correlation with openness to experience and neuroticism (Power and Pluess 2015). Knowing your level of openness, extroversion, and neuroticism affect how you view yourself as a communicator and how you communicate naturally with other people in different settings.

For example, the level of conscientiousness impacts the amount of discipline and detail toward message preparation and practice; neuroticism affects the level of assertiveness and can be abrasive; and openness to experience and the level of extraversion impact the willingness to communicate and how often in a variety of circumstances. Ultimately, the speaker can shift from an existing limited mindset based on self-perception: "Because I'm this (i.e., introverted), I can't do that (i.e., speak)" to "I'm open to new experiences and trust my ability."

CORE VALUES INFLUENCE COMMUNICATION

Our core values, those traits and qualities that represent our beliefs and priorities, affect how we communicate with others. The most memorable speakers align to their beliefs. Some speakers communicate excitedly, keyed and pumped up—never feeling a dull moment. They perform to make an impact on people. These speakers display a strong presence, want something to happen, and make a mark with their words. Think Tony Robbins, Erin Brockovich, or Muhammad Ali.

Other speakers show more concern, dependability, vested in a sense of belonging. They communicate in civic groups and committees to make things happen in their community with steadfast trustworthiness. Think Jimmy Carter, Harry S. Truman, or Rosa Parks.

Other speakers bubble up with enthusiasm, quick to feel and express emotions, warm and loving, with boundless intensity with ideas and insights, inspiring others. Think Nelson Mandela, Martin Luther King Jr., or Oprah Winfrey.

Some speakers display a calm, cool, and collected energy, particularly in stressful situations. Their value for accuracy, logic, and strategic responses may affect their intensity. Their curiosity and inquisitive, investigative spirit inspire their message. Think Abraham Lincoln, Hilary Clinton, or Steve Jobs.

As you craft your next message, tune into your core values. What you believe and what you feel affect what you say.

COMMITMENT TO SPEAK AND TRAINING INCREASE MAGNETISM

In a 2022 Captivate workshop, speaking coach Suzanne Evans stresses we're born demanding, not captivating. Furthermore, she expresses the captivating speaker's responsibility to balance their beliefs with their brain and body. Training proves to be what matters most to improve communication skills. A study evaluates the Big Five Personality Traits with mastering communication skills, specifically assertiveness (Kuntze, van der Molen, and Born 2016). The researchers discover practice predicts a more significant improvement with performance than personality traits. Participants who receive direct communication training showed the most progress.

Psychologist Dr. Kim Hoogeveen says, "You obviously can't do anything you want, but when you combine hard work with some modicum of natural ability you can accelerate what you do well." Dr. Hoogeveen illustrates everyone cannot be a neurosurgeon, the fastest runner, or best golfer, yet individuals can improve their current talent by making the decision to do so by taking time to practice. He says, "What looks like skill to others is often just a lot of work no one sees. Long nights, early mornings. If you want to be great, you have to grind; it's actually all that hard work that makes it look easy." What we choose to concentrate on grows our internal confidence, skill ability, and builds on behavioral patterns. When I started my business, I improved my virtual presentations by committing to co-facilitating monthly workshops online rather than avoiding technology altogether. Magnetic speakers improve their talent choosing to do so and through work.

Echoing Dr. Hoogeveen, Associate Professor Kevin Mitchell states in a podcast, "[...] We are inevitably born with some differences [...] That doesn't necessarily mean that our patterns of behavior are fixed. Those are just underlying predispositions, and then they inform our behavior somewhat [...] if someone is slightly risk averse, that's going to affect their behavior over their lifetime in a statistical sense" (Mitchell 2022). Brian Drury, international speaker and presentation trainer, explains there's a difference between having the desire to speak on a stage and being able to speak effectively. Some personalities may have a deeper desire to speak, and Drury expounds, with enough work, anyone can learn the art of public speaking.

Environment plays a role in the ability to be magnetic. A study researches personality development, exploring both environmental factors and genetics in personality trait changes from the beginning of a person's life to their transition into adulthood (Hopwood et al. 2011). Their research suggests genetic factors are important for understanding personality stability and change, yet environmental factors matter in a person's growth, shaping their disposition and skill level. If leaders offer novice speakers on their team opportunities to speak and encourage them to do so (providing the environment), the individual can increase their confidence and improve their communication skills.

However, we can overestimate our ability. Dr. Hoogeveen discusses this cognitive bias concept of illusory superiority. He says, "People will not delude themselves as to their ability when it comes to things that are easy to measure or evaluate (e.g., running a mile under five minutes or singing well); whereas, with things that are hard to measure (e.g., driving, leadership, teaching and speaking skills) they will often overestimate their ability." We can, however, enact new and different personality traits to complete a project and act out of character because of stress or context.

Theatre professor Gretta Berghammer says, "I know I can tell a good story and be funny. When it comes to the qualities of magnetic speaking, some are innate, but that doesn't mean they can't be learned. Some individuals are naturally more expressive, born storytellers, more comfortable speaking, while some are witty and have a sense of humor. All can be learned and used." She stresses the more genuine and experienced speakers exude confidence. If the speaker matches their talents and individual style, create heart-centered material, and practice the skill, they spark magnetism.

What talents carry you? What do you want your audience to know, do, and potentially feel when you're done with the presentation? The speaker needs to balance this tension. Berghammer emphasizes, "Everybody brings something to the podium as a speaker." Magnetic speakers believe this ideal and select the most effective approach. They use appropriate visual aids and have an appealing vocal and physical delivery. Inborn personality traits can attract the frequency to seek out more opportunities to speak. Yet, the commitment to learn with informed guidance from a coach increases the possibility to craft engaging content and perform with dynamic delivery.

Magnetic speaking can be learned and refined through rehearsal.

SPEAKING STRATEGIES TO REACH DIFFERENT PERSONALITIES

Dr. McKenna illustrates how he teaches college students with different personality types. He has two options to direct student learning. Option 1: Lecture three times a week. Students take notes and midterm exams are based on lectures. The exams reflect the professor's viewpoint, not allowing student input. Option 2: Create an open class, invite students to talk, break them into small groups with guidance, and respond to their questions. While his preference is option one, he adjusts his teaching style to give students more engagement. Dr. McKenna says, "I become the teacher students need me to be. Leadership is not always directive—it's sharing." He alters his preferred teaching style to best meet the needs of his students for them to learn, grow, and engage.

To be truly magnetic, speakers explore performance and presentation styles. What's important to the audience and their varied core values? Using different styles attracts and engages audiences to listen and the message to resonate.

Tina's Tips to Connect with Different Personality Types

Be Credible: Aristotle highlights the importance of logos, ethos, and pathos. Balancing these three elements builds a more effective message. Clear structure and research establish your credibility. Citing relevant, relatable, and timely sources develops your authority on the subject. Some audience members dismiss your content if you fail to provide data or demonstrate your expertise. Display your authority on the topic.

Be Engaging to Make an Impact: Audiences appreciate opportunities to participate. Request the audience to call out examples, raise their hands, discuss a concept or question with partners, or use props and activities aligning to your speaking objective. While this may not be at the forefront of what's important to you (for example, researching information and sharing knowledge might be), the audience craves engagement and witnessing the speaker's enjoyment.

Be Unique and Authentic: The audience wants the real you. Express emotions and share stories in your unique voice and style. Some audience members may feel betrayed if you fail to show vulnerability. Perhaps you sing a portion of your keynote, pop on a signature costume piece during a workshop, or provide a funny comic or joke at the beginning of each team meeting. Understand and capitalize your individualized preferences to captivate the room.

Establish a Connection: Speak with your audience, not "to" or "at" them. "With" personifies audience-centeredness. Make the exchange more of a conversation. Refer to the specific group or organization and use pronouns, "we," "us," and "you." Include timely, relevant examples to support your main points. Be aware of you and your audience's spectrum of emotions. Establish rapport, maintain it, and show you care.

Is speaking magnetic hard? Scary? Does it take time? It can be, yet all of us have the ability to be magnetic. Conscious communicators think about their content with the audience at the top of mind and heart. Nancy Duarte states it takes strategy, delivery, story, empathy, and visuals to connect with an audience, and that can be taught and learned (Duarte 2023). Strive to comprehend the other and adjust your style to meet the audience preferences. Shift from the Golden Rule, "Do unto others as you would have done unto you," to the Silver Rule, "Do unto others as they would like to have done unto them."

Knowing who you are affects how you work, communicate, and lead.

EXERCISES

Take a personality test to become more self-aware (Myers-Briggs, Keirsey Temperament, Enneagram, Emergenetics, Predictive Index, Colors, DISC, etc.). Read the responses on the assessment. Ask yourself what feels true. What doesn't? Ask others (both personally and professionally) to share their experience of you and note their feedback without emotions attached.

Assess a past presentation. Reflect on what you said, how you communicated the message, and the audience's responses. Did you balance credibility and engagement strategies as your authentic self? What worked and was natural for you? Where can you see an area of growth?

Plan your next presentation. Do what's hard first. If "fun" is the last thing on your mind, start there. Ask yourself: How can I develop a fun presentation to absorb the audience's attention? Involve their participation with an activity or bring an audience member on stage. Explore different.

REFLECTION QUESTIONS

Do I show my personality when speaking?

Do I see myself as a magnetic speaker? If not, how do I perceive myself as a speaker? What's holding me back?

Evaluate your temperament and Big Five Personality Traits. How does that affect and influence my communication?

Was my recent presentation/communication engaging? Did I balance credibility of content and knowledge with story?

Did audience members ask me questions? Speak with me following my presentation?

Of the four speaking strategies, which is easiest for me? Which is hardest?

What strings are keeping me down, tethering my balloon to magnetic greatness?

MAGNETIC SPEAKERS ARE AUTHENTIC

---

*You don't have to change who you are; you
have to become more of who you are.*

—SALLY HOGSHEAD, AUTHOR, SPEAKER

"Authenticity is magnetic."

—UNKNOWN

A bright spotlight shines directly in my eyes as I utter my first
line for a storytelling show on a small, wooden platform in
a rural cafe. I've convinced the owner to host a storytelling
event, including a professional storyteller from New York.

I request to perform first. My overwhelming jitters take over
my body. The wave of sheer terror sinks deeply as my heart
throbs outside of my chest. I know I've made a mistake. For
the first time in my life, I memorize my story.

Every.

Single.

Word.

I've always told my clients, "Do not, under any circumstances, memorize your story. Know how you're going to start, know how you're going to end, and your basic structure in the middle. Then, trust yourself."

I don't trust myself.

Going through the memorized motions in a robotic trance, I present, rather than share my story. Because I have a theatre background, it's going well. I'm faking it.

Faking it hard.

A woman's cell phone rings boldly, blatantly, and without remorse. Experiencing this performer's nightmare, I pause. The shrill rings drown out my voice.

Once the blaring rings finally mute, I wonder, "Where am I in the story?" Panicked shivers surge through my spine and throat. I think, "Just breathe. Relax. The story will come." With a lengthy pause and breath, I choke out the final words on autopilot. The audience's responses don't feel fulfilling. After the applause, I sense zero gratification from this performance.

Fast forward four days later. I'm relaxed, in full after-glow of a successful week of professional workshops and coaching.

The emcee calls my name. I step forward to the microphone. Animated and self-assured, my bright voice projects the first line. The audience squeals loud laughter throughout, beams large smiles, claps, and the performance ends with a standing ovation. Elated at this different experience, the reactions mean far more this time. I bubble with joyful enthusiasm.

My story isn't memorized. I let go of my theatrical autopilot mode. This time, my words matter—to me. And, it feels good. Really good.

What's the difference between these two speaking performances? My conditioned self performs weighted in worry of others' judgments and fear of failure. The second performance I emerge full force, energized with faith in my authentic self. Instead of presenting the story, I share from the heart and let my knowing guide me word for word.

What influences my different way of being, from a lack-luster performance to a fully heart-centered one?

I initiate the idea of a storytelling show with the restaurant owner and place unnecessary pressure for the show to be a booming success. My former beloved elementary teacher, 4-H leader, mother, and other important women in my life sit in the crowd. I wear the deep desire for achievement and burden of heavy expectations on my shoulders.

The second performance exhibits a completely different mindset and experience: I present to a high school audience with a clear mind. The lower pressure to succeed boosts my self-trust. Relying on my past rehearsals to work, I stand on stage and speak from the heart. I believe in myself; it's my experience, my story. I went from thinking or believing I could do it to truly knowing.

WHAT DOES IT MEAN TO BE "AUTHENTIC?"

The word "authentic" comes from the Greek word "authentikos," which means "original, genuine, principal" (Etymology Dictionary 2023). Professor Herminia Ibarra addresses identity in her TEDx Talk and defines authenticity as being sincere and true to the self and your values (Ibarra 2018). Psychologists have researched the concept of authenticity, specifically Abraham Maslow's pyramid of needs which focuses on achieving self-actualization. Maslow acknowledges becoming your own person, a best version of yourself, isn't a trait, but a process (Ibarra 2018).

Ryan Smerek, PhD, defines authenticity as the "congruence between our deeper values and beliefs and actions" (2021). To be an "authentic speaker," communication coach Emma Serlin says it's "making the listener see what it is that you see and feel what you feel [...] speaking about a topic you are passionate about, your body will engage, your eyes will brighten, and your voice will be powered by your breath" (2015).

Authentic speakers communicate with a real, natural, and original style. Using my creative spirit as a high school cafe server, I labeled desserts descriptive names like "Zesty Zucchini Cake" and "Sensational Strawberry Pie." As a teacher, I developed entertaining theatre activities to attract high school students to learn Shakespeare and college students to study communication theory. Even in my nonprofit and for-profit positions, I promoted the arts through stories and puppetry to build a rapport within my rural community.

WHAT OTHER PROFESSIONALS SAY ABOUT
BEING AN AUTHENTIC SPEAKER:
* * *Primary interviews from professionals regarding speaking

"The message is real for you, not thin and watery. It's thought through, important, and has value, a well-developed idea that honestly has value to others without being me-centered."

—JUDE TREDER-WOLFF, PSYCHOTHERAPIST,
WRITER/PERFORMER

"It's hard for me to define—not selling out. It's being a leader more than an entertainer, making an impact. Authenticity shows in people who have worked to be authentic."

—ERIK DOMINGUEZ, COMMUNICATION CONSULTANT

"[The speaker has] done the work, emotionally arrived with the material, and reframed it. It helped them, so they want to help others with why we exist in the world."

—MARY SWANDER, AGARTS EXECUTIVE DIRECTOR, AUTHOR

"Stand in your truth. Be yourself. Find your voice."

—FRANK KING, COMEDIAN, KEYNOTE SPEAKER

Recently, I read *Jonathan Livingston Seagull,* which explores authenticity (Bach 2014). This fable follows Jonathan's flights of leaving the flock and his exploration into the fearless, unlimited self (Bach 2014, 17-26). Loving the self, feeling free, and experiencing joy come from expressing our true nature.

As Jonathan announces to the other gulls, "We're free to go where we wish and be who we are" (Bach 2014, 75). Jonathan Livingston Seagull teaches me to see myself, feel it, trust it, and be it. "Authentic" is a condition of being in a constant state of unfolding. Magnetic speakers have the courage to relate in an honest way with themselves and their audience.

LETTING GO OF THE CONDITIONED SELF

With the rise of social media, people use the word "authentic" frequently. Author Bo Lozoff states to focus on love and though our circumstances and environments are not in our control, the ability to choose inner faith and love always is (1999, 100). During my holistic psychology certification process, I learn a distinction between the authentic versus the conditioned self from holistic psychotherapist Shelley Riutta (2021). She stresses we must treat ourselves as loving, wise adults. Riutta created the list below, contrasting attributes of the conditioned self and authentic self.

"CONDITIONED SELF VERSUS AUTHENTIC SELF

Fear versus Faith

Lack of fulfillment versus Full of purpose

Holding back/staying small versus Taking positive, consistent action

Worrying about others' judgments versus Inspired self-confidence

Negative thinking versus Positive/optimistic thinking

Constricted thinking versus Expansive thinking
Weighed down and heavy energy versus Light and
freeing energy

Feeling like a victim versus Feeling empowered
Seeing only barriers versus Seeing endless possibilities"

(RIUTTA 2021)

We create our circumstances by the stories we tell ourselves. Our core stories determine the level of enoughness we feel and express. Psychotherapist Shelley Riutta says, "You're the driver of the bus." She stresses the importance of the loving, wise adult that drives our thoughts, feelings, and decisions, not our five-year-old self, teenage-self, or the part of us that's hurt, insecure, or broken.

Irrational beliefs link to negative experiences, and emotions influence our behavior and communication. Psychologist and cognitive theorist Albert Ellis explains, to change thinking, the individual must identify the activating event, the attached belief, and observe the consequences (Nevid, Rathus, and Greene 2012, 152). Our cognitive constructs lead either to speaking apprehension or positive experience in future communication and shape a person's verbal ability.

Aristotle defines the human psyche as being responsible for our consciousness, perceptions, and emotions. What we're aware of, how we see things, and react, all matter with how we relate to other people. Magnetic communicators have what Suzanne Kobasa calls "psychological hardiness," a level of grit and knowledge we have control over our circumstances and reactions to respond to people appropriately (Nevid, Rathus, and Greene 2012, 152-155). The ability to cope with difficult people and behave and communicate skillfully with emotional intelligence produce positive results. If a conflict arises or the unexpected occurs, the magnetic communicator pauses, labels the moment for what it is, then relates to others appropriately in the given context.

Psychology Today author Theo Tsaousides, PhD, analyzes conquering the internal fear through cognitive reframing of what you believe about speaking, shifting the focus from performance to communication, and seeking out more opportunities to speak (2017). Changing the conditioned self-mindset requires practicing faith rather than fear-focused internal talk. We must modify our speaking patterns when our thinking and energy do not align. For example, if a speaker is thinking ahead of what they're going to say, not listening to the other, or over-talking, these behaviors indicate either the ego or self-doubt are sneaking in and taking over. Pause, move into the mindset of the authentic self, then respond.

A study finds cumulative childhood trauma associates higher rates of adult psychiatric disorders and poorer functional outcomes, including transition to adulthood, failure to hold a job, and social isolation (Copeland et al. 2018). These findings echo Dr. Gabor Mate's research. He explains if a child experiences trauma they're more likely to experience pain as an adult (Mate 2023). These traumatic experiences can influence the individual's thinking, self-talk, view of self, and communication patterns as the conditioned self. Dr. Mate emphasizes exploring why you're a certain way with compassionate curiosity (2023). We're all born complete.

Introspection and self-thought can be inaccurate. Psychologist Tasha Eurich analyzes how introspective people get caught in ruminative patterns, particularly when they receive corrective feedback (2018). Eurich notes not to rush our reaction, gather more data to assess the accuracy, and be open to change. Additionally, when we ask "why," it centers on conditioned, fear-based beliefs, weaknesses, and insecurities and impacts communication style. The better question is asking "what." Explore your internal thoughts and external behaviors and seek out answers to what you can do and request honest and accurate feedback from a caring colleague for support. I've heard there are three types of speeches: the one you prepare, the one you give, and the one you wish you'd given. Spend less time focusing on the one you wish you would have given (that's the conditioned self talking) and more time on your success and accomplishment of completing the speech as the authentic self.

The more we love ourselves, the more we love others, the more others feel our love. Whether it's with our words or just being in a space, others feel it. I traveled on a solo trip to Atlanta to write this book, without an agenda other than being fully present and exploring art. While waiting for a table, a restaurant server, unsolicited, approaches and says, "I can feel your strong aura. You are magnetic. I felt I needed to tell you." I haven't said a word. In an inner state of self-love, my presence connects with her at a deeper level.

Powerful magnetism originates within.

BENEFITS OF BEING AUTHENTIC

Authenticity connects you with your audience.

My client Meg cares about sharing her story on the TED stage. Yet, her story explores extremely personal and emotional challenges, as she continues to process her diagnosis of epilepsy. We collaborate and develop her TEDx Talk, walking through each part of the speech.

I say, "You need to feel it. Really feel it. Cry. Talk though the words and feel your story more."

For her to present authentically and reach her audience without breaking down midway, she needs emotional support and guidance. Meg communicates her feelings first. She develops an intense, audience-centered TEDx presentation, which includes rich clarity about her epilepsy journey, losing her nursing position, and creating the nonprofit Camp You-Can. If we created the content without addressing her feelings, the final speech wouldn't have been as authentic or impactful.

Authenticity demands digging in and feeling the pain. Meg reveals her mindset along the way. She's open about her journey and continuous growth. She transports the audience on a voyage from her past pain to her present grief. Her current state of mind, a hope for the future, generates audience tears and resounding applause. She focuses on her audience, drawing them into her transformational mindset as she leads with feelings first. The compassionate, guided practice along the way pushes her to believe she can present a compelling talk. Meg transitions out of her conditioned self of fearing she'll forget parts of the speech (a realistic condition resulting from her brain surgery) to disclose her TEDx Talk as her true, authentic self.

Authenticity increases confidence and grows business.

Another client, youthful aging advocate and thriving entrepreneur, Cynthia, approaches me, feeling issues with perfectionism and negative thoughts of not being good enough.

In a coaching session, Cynthia says, "Who's going to listen to me?" "Who's going to want what I have to offer?" She exclaims she feels fear, restricted, and desires freedom. She aspires to believe in herself and her business.

I say, "Let go of how others perceive your looks and voice. Instead, focus on being fully present and feel the space and moment for what it is then trust your words will appear."

After a mindset shift, plenty of practice, and three months of guided support, she experiences a "180-degree flip." Cynthia says, "Now, I'm attracting others because I have that confidence and belief that I have something worth sharing." She releases the fear and concentrates on being her authentic self.

Authenticity lessens stress and improves relationships.

Communication coach Nick Morgan states, "Authenticity—including the ability to communicate authentically with others—has become an important leadership attribute. When leaders have it, they can inspire their followers to make extraordinary efforts on behalf of their organizations. When they don't, cynicism prevails, and few employees do more than the minimum necessary to get by" (2008). Being authentic is having an openness with your audience, fully connecting with yourself, your topic, and the space. When you're fully present as the self, listen to your audience's verbal and nonverbal reactions, you'll witness rich responses, desired outcomes, and feel empowered.

In one study, participants assess their Big Five Personality Traits and respond to questions regarding how authentic they feel in different roles, ranging from employee to friend (Wood et al. 2008). Authentic speakers are satisfied in a role rank being less neurotic, experience less stress, anxiety, and depression, and have higher self-esteem. Additionally, they express feeling relatively more conscientious, agreeable, and open to experience.

Another study correlates authentic living with a higher self-esteem, more positive emotions, and increased happiness (Sheldon et al. 1997). Authentic-identified participants report increased personal growth and experience healthier relationships. As I've stretched into my authentic self, I've seen my business income grow and my professional and personal relationships blossom.

THE CHALLENGE OF AUTHENTICITY

Balancing authenticity with audience engagement can challenge speakers. Professor Herminia Ibarra discusses the authenticity paradox in her TEDx Talk (Ibarra 2018). She defines this paradox as "what got you here won't get you there." Ibarra explains the importance of doing what's effective may mean altering your true self, citing the example of improving her past appalling teaching style. Years ago, I witnessed a researcher present a data-loaded speech. The presenter clicks from one chart to the next. Numbers dominate, without a story in sight. During the speaker's presentation, audience members shift in their seats, stare, and tap their cell phone screens, and whisper to their neighbors. This presenter exhibits authenticity. Unfortunately, the presenter's deep value for data and highly complex, analytical style fail to reach the audience. The speaker's rigidity affects the impact of the message.

Social psychologist and TED speaker Brené Brown embodies authenticity. Her TED talks on difficult topics of vulnerability and shame have more than twenty-two million views. Brown dresses comfortably in clogs and jean skirts to fit her style, speaks in a conversational tone (even cusses occasionally), and appears at ease on any stage. Over time, I've evolved my speaker style to match my authentic self. When I speak, I share more personal stories, use props, and have rid my closet of stoic suits. Authenticity, however, can come with heavy consequences. A woman choosing to wear a burka despite expectations she should wear dress pants and a blazer may be more likely to experience a negative reaction from the audience due to racism/Islamophobia, regardless of how authentic she feels.

You've heard the term "fake it till you make it." Yet, social psychologist Amy Cuddy coins the phrase, "fake it till you become it" in her TED talk (Cuddy 2012). At times, I've tricked my brain and voice into "becoming it." From stepping into a college lecture hall for the first time as a new instructor to presenting on a TEDx stage, to facilitating my first online improvisation workshop, I've faced the fear and confronted my limiting, conditioned beliefs to embrace my true, authentic self.

Take the Authentic Self Path

Path 1: The conditioned self victim lives and communicates with fear and heavy energy.

Path 2: The conditioned self people-pleaser communicates what they think others want them to say, act, and be.

Path 3: The authentic self stays present in their being no matter the given circumstances, feeling loved, valued, and enough.

Every human has a flavor of not enough. Use your original language, vocal, physical, and appearance choices that feel right and true to you. Ask yourself: Is my preparation enough? How much practice is enough to feel like myself? Notice your frequent thinking and speech patterns. Set the intention to slow down and pause your mind. Breathe, and the body will take you there.

Suspend self-judgment, trust and allow the process to unfold.

TINA'S TIPS TO SHIFT FROM YOUR CONDITIONED SELF TO YOUR AUTHENTIC SELF

Moving out of your conditioned self is a choice. These ideas transition your energy:

> Express appreciation for others; write a list of successes, gratitudes, and celebrations (Riutta 2021).

Watch a funny video or call a friend who makes you laugh.

Read inspirational books, articles, and quotes.

Listen to motivational music; dance to your favorite song.

Meditate; walk in nature.

Ask yourself: What would be loving for me right now? (Riutta 2021)

EXERCISE

Document your level of confidence. Where am I in this moment?

Today, I feel _____

My confidence level on a scale from one to ten
(ten = super confident) _____

I am aware _____ is affecting my confidence.

What are you focusing on? Successes or failures? List current successes worth celebrating.

What are you saying to yourself? Our inner chatter affects our view of self and behavior.

List three common thoughts you say to yourself. Replace negative thoughts with positive.

1.

2.

3.

Envision your next level of confidence. What is unique about you? Reflect on a specific time where you felt your best. What made you feel the best? Describe what a magnetic speaker looks like for you, using words to describe the behaviors and attributes. Picture this person completely. Step into the new identity. Ask yourself: *Who do I need to be to achieve this?* Cultivate and create this identity and anchor into your authentic self. Now write a sentence embodying the belief of what you described.

What are three steps to seek your adventurous speaking goal?

1.

2.

3.

How will you be the authentic speaker you are? What will you wear? Say? Behave?

**Sometimes your identity can be a mirror covered with dust. Clear the mirror to find and witness your true reflection, your magnetic self. Be you, for everyone else is taken.

REFLECTION QUESTIONS

What are my limiting beliefs/mindsets?

What are two to three conditioned self behaviors I'd like to improve to embody my authentic self?

What's a past story that has affected my communication style or has defined me?

What is one new story I'd like to envision and tell myself?

What strategies will get me out of my conditioned self?

Journal this week, noting when you're in your conditioned self and when you're in your authentic self. Explore your triggers (consistent times of day, people, energy levels, stress, etc., that affect your way of being).

CONNECT AND COMMUNICATE IN A MAGNETIC STYLE

Communication is not about speaking what we think.
Communication is ensuring others will hear what we mean.

—TED SPEAKER, AUTHOR SIMON SINEK

Know thyself.

—PLATO

I have a confession to make. I'm an ultra-sensitive, thoughtful introvert stuck in an extrovert's body.

What does this mean?

I prefer to coach or consult, support the speaker rather than perform on stage. My passion for performance comes from the enjoyment of viewing it, experiencing it, assessing it, and educating others of best communication practices.

Most people who know me think I'm a powerhouse extrovert. Even in a statewide leadership class, I identify as the most extroverted person in a room of forty people. With careful research and observation, I prefer rich, deep, one-on-one conversations and long periods of quiet, inner reflection. In the past, I've overcompensated my need for quiet, alone time to think, ponder, and distill information with loud, big bursts of vocal and physical energy in large groups.

The terms "introvert" and "extrovert" receive a ridiculous amount of attention. Humans love labels. We're curious about who we are and aspire to understand why we and others do what we do. Hence, why we've taken a wide range of assessments, from Myers-Briggs to Emergenetics, to CliftonStrengths or Predictive Index.

Psychology researcher Elaine Houston defines introvert as being directed inward with a higher desire for thought over social experiences; whereas, the extrovert has more outward interest in social environments with less desire for detailed observation (2019). Houston continues to explain the ambivert flexes between the two styles, exhibiting behaviors and qualities of both (Houston 2019). Unlike the easy, identifiable physical characteristics (i.e., hair color), introversion and extroversion attributes are internal and affected by the individual's energetic needs. Energy, along with the environment, influence behavior.

People confuse introversion with shyness. The American Psychological Association defines shy as "the tendency to feel awkward, worried, or tense during social encounters, especially with unfamiliar people" (2023). Shy people suffer from intense negative feelings about themselves, may experience severe physical symptoms, and withdrawing from social interactions, whereas introverts do not have as intense negative feelings and responses. Instead, introverts simply need quiet reflection and alone time to charge their batteries. Extroverts, on the other hand, amp up their energy with people.

Communications and leadership visionary AlexSandra Leslie, who has coached thousands of keynote speakers, describes in an interview, introverts characteristically find being magnetic is out of their comfort zone. Introverts regulate inward and think quietly in their minds without a need to speak out. Extroverts, however, need to speak out and express themselves as part of their style. Leslie explains everyone is absolutely capable of being magnetic, and introverts can do so by using what Leslie refers to as PEARLS: pictures, examples, analogies, references, levity, and stories. She says, "Find your enthusiasm for the topic, and then meet the needs of the audience as you deliver it. Ask yourself, 'Why are they here? What are they looking for?'"

Leslie shares a story about an introverted engineer who stands still when he speaks, nervous and uncomfortable, just trying to get through his content. When he sees the impact he has on his audiences, he realizes the need to become more dynamic and focus more on the audience and less on himself. Together, with Leslie's help, he starts using compelling stories, creative visuals, and analogies to be more relatable. From seeing audience feedback and comparing himself to other speakers, he learns to express other parts of himself.

Introverts can draw from their strengths, learn, and practice strategies to engage audiences.

While introverts may be reticent to speak and lack the desire to step in front of people to express their ideas, with guidance and concentrated work using elements of powerful and dynamic presentations, they can get much more comfortable speaking publicly. Leslie describes those elements as the four v's: *verbal, vocal,* and *visual* components of the message, along with the speaker's personal *vitality.*

Although I've performed in speech competitions, community theatre, and storytelling shows, I'm terrified and dying inside every time prior and during. Launching my business Tina B. LLC, I notice my inner introvert. With a forced intensity to grow and market my business, the talking to people every day depletes my energy. Apprehensive, I hold my breath. My heart races as I talk faster. Exhausted with each verbal exchange, I collapse like a limp noodle into bed at the end of each day. For me, networking is overwhelming. The large space of humming conversations and noisy, clanging glasses contrast with my need to connect deeply even though I can't attend to everyone. I know this feat is impossible. For some, this scenario is natural and exciting. For many, including me, it's not.

Through self-exploration of my communication style, I'm what psychologist Elaine Aron calls a highly sensitive person (HSP) (Aron 2016, 8-11). My brain goes into overdrive when overstimulated. I jump at shrill noises and jolt in large crowds of people, feeling all their energy. Additionally, I project rich empathy for people and sense others' energy with my intuition. Noticing the slightest subtleties in environments (a small increase in temperature or lowered lighting) and people's behaviors (facial expressions) are my superpowers.

We observe, react, connect, and communicate with others in the world differently. From a Daoist perspective, spiritual guide Bill Schaefer has defined each person has a reaction type: body, heart, or mind (2015). Maybe you're the type of person who reacts from the gut, knowing right from wrong and how to engage with a situation or person. While another person feels deeply and takes on other's emotions as their own yet struggling to feel theirs. Or perhaps you're analytical and think first in terms of concepts and philosophies, and then engage in the world.

How can we "get" others and be gotten? We can become the label we see, hear, and use most. Being extroverted or introverted is such a small sliver of who we are. We need to advocate for our energetic needs to be the best we can be in each communication. It's essential to identify time for rest, times of play, transitions from meetings, and amount of daily people encounters. Each individual's energy and needs vary. When I present a keynote or facilitate a workshop, I block off time the day prior and following to recoup. I also limit people meetings to three a day to provide spaciousness to think and gain energy.

Prior or after speaking, ask: What do I need in this moment? How can I best connect with myself to relate at a deeper level with an individual, team, or larger audience, and communicate a style most true to me? Interpreting the self, needs, and wants has a dramatic impact on the psyche and presentation.

All this discussion matters because whether you're shy, a sensitive extrovert, ambivert, louder introvert who's had to overcompensate to earn merits at work, or you vary your style each day based on the context, you can become self-aware and use strategies to communicate more effectively. From Zoom calls to proposing a new idea to your team, or winning a prospective client, we all have the capacity to be magnetic. Practicing strategies helps express your ideas clearly and build stronger relationships.

COMMUNICATE FOR RESULTS: IDENTIFY COMMUNICATION STYLE

The amount of words we speak, to whom, and how often are influenced by our preferences and internal energy. "Communication style indicates how a person structures the world of social relations" (Dhillon and Kaur 2021). Researcher Cheryl Hamilton defines four communication styles: closed, blind, hidden, and open (2011, 69-75). She breaks down the four communication styles by how individuals balance the amount of self-disclosure with feedback. The American Psychological Association defines self-disclosure as "the act of revealing personal or private information about one's self to other people and fosters feelings of closeness and intimacy" (2023). This definition includes the amount and depth of information an individual feels comfortable sharing. Feedback is the response an audience has to a message or activity (Nordquist 2019).

"Closed: low self-disclosure and low feedback
Blind: high self-disclosure and low feedback
Hidden: low self-disclosure and high feedback
Open: high self-disclosure and high feedback"

(HAMILTON 2011, 69-75)

We have communication preferences, yet context matters. For example, my default communication pattern is open. I'm most authentic when I connect with people, ask questions to learn more about others, and reveal information about myself. Yet, I have shifted to the other styles when I'm uncomfortable in the speaking context, need more information, or my physical state of being isn't at its best. Humans are driven by energy. Our level of trust we share when meeting someone new or enthusiasm we feel when we experience different impacts the communicative response.

What amount of self-disclosure feels comfortable, and what amount of feedback will you accept and communicate with others?

Hamilton defines a closed communicator as having the preference to work with things, not people (2011, 69). As a master carpenter, my father-in-law loves burying himself in his work rather than communicating with others. With art, he prefers creating and giving it away. Ask him to discuss his process, and his eyes light up. He describes with clarity his creative methods. Being curious in his interests, his closed style, preference for working with things, softens, and he opens up.

Closed communicators struggle to engage in small talk. To connect with closed communicators:

Speak about systems, concepts, processes.

Discuss topics they know and care about.

Be purposeful and listen.

Ask them specific questions about their work
or project.

Hamilton explains a blind communicator prefers to communicate their knowledge and express what they know about a topic (2011, 71). During a past networking event, an individual talked about a project and made the exchange all about their ideas and plan, failing to request feedback or engagement from me. I've transformed into this style when I seek approval, know a concept, or let my ego take over.

To connect with blind communicators:

Be purposeful with your comments.

Ask thoughtful questions to build on the
conversation.

Get curious; they appreciate creative contributions
to the conversation.

Muse on theories and possibilities highlighting
and supporting their expertise.

Hamilton defines the hidden communicator as having a preference to listen and ask questions, getting to know the other person, while discussing very little about themselves (2011, 73). My first year teaching at a university, I transitioned into the hidden style due to zero experience in academia. I listened, inquired, and focused on learning my colleagues' work and communication style to support them. Fear of hurting my credibility, I probed professors for information. Eventually, with time and growing comfort, I balanced my amount of sharing and listening in department meetings.

To connect with hidden communicators:

Appreciate their active listening, but don't abuse it.

Start with low levels of self-disclosure and low-risk questions to build trust.

Ask for their feedback.

Share your information, and then provide follow-up questions.

Hamilton explains open communicators prefer expressing information about the self and asking others to share about themselves (2011, 75). This style can be too much for people, both with content and body language. Open communicators mustn't invade personal space nor speak too much. Prior to presenting, I normally take five minutes alone to prepare; however, before one presentation, an audience member promptly talks to me. My nervous energy takes over. I move into the individual's personal space with a thunderous voice and bigger gestures. The person locks eyes with someone else across the room and quickly shuffles in that direction communicating the conversation has concluded. Though we have a positive conversation following my presentation, this experience reminds me to give space for myself and others.

To connect with open communicators:

Be balanced and tune into your and the other's energy.

Be aware many open communicators fail to have a bubble and may invade personal space.

Communicate with clarity and request what you want and need.

Show interest in what they have to say.

We can stay on autopilot, ignoring the issue, rather than stepping into the discomfort and communicate. Executive leadership coach Sarah Noll Wilson labels this behavior as the "avoid-aphant," which may lead to potential conflict (2022, 67). Take notice of the context and note your communication style and comprehend others have preferences and different energy levels. Self-assess: Are you more direct, dominating in making decisions and requests, or are you more collaborative, creating harmony and finding a solution for everyone? Do you consider yourself more of an influencer who's a visionary and gets to the "why" (Emerson 2022)? Having honest awareness of your style comes from clear evaluation of the context and listening to feedback. Then, adapt.

One study assesses teacher's communication style and notes teacher style has impact on their communication effectiveness with students (Dhillon and Kaur 2021). Teachers conduct self-assessments and refer to how they receive and give information. Levels of "expressiveness" and "preciseness" influence the instructor's outlook on sharing knowledge and their student relationships. In contrast, the study finds verbal aggressiveness creates an "inverse relationship" with their effectiveness in teaching. The researchers emphasize the need for self-assessment to enhance communication effectiveness, demonstrate competence, and expand interpersonal relationships (Dhillon and Kaur 2021).

Additionally, know your apprehension style. Communication researchers Steven Beebe and Susan Beebe explain the need to be audience-centered in the speech-making process requires clarity, delivery style, and awareness of your apprehension style (2010, 9-10). Are you confrontational, inflexible, insensitive, or an average speaker? Each of these styles improve with preparation and calming techniques prior, during, and following communication.

COMMUNICATION CHANNEL PREFERENCES

We all have preferences guiding what channel we use to communicate with one another. Some prefer in-person communication, while others are more suited for written or online. Examine what your style preference is, and then acknowledge your communication channel preference may not be the same as someone else's. Understanding we're different is at the center of our experience. Dr. John McKenna says, "If we can get beyond our preferences, react differently to others based on theirs, adjusting our style, we'll see better connection."

Some people prefer online communication because it's more efficient and less personal, while others may like in-person meetings to relate with others. Even how we show up nonverbally matters and differs. Some people are tuned into the energy of the space and person, and everything means something. A change in facial expressions, gestures, and tone of voice affect their interpretation of the message, whereas other individuals hear the message and need more direct communication to comprehend what is said. Some may see what a person is wearing and if it's too traditional or jazzy, the outfit may be the focus of the exchange and distract from the message.

Dr. McKenna cites two questions to ask prior to each communication:

How can I best impact others?

What do you see in others that impacts you?

Everyone has a hardwired, preferred style. This awareness helps us better comprehend what others say or fail to say, or show or fail to show emotionally. Our overall speaking style varies. If we adjust our communication style, even if it isn't our preference, we'll move the conversation forward for better comprehension.

ADAPTING COMMUNICATION STYLE
IN PERSON AND ONLINE

To connect with others may require modifying your communication style preference and work a new muscle. As an open communicator, I read the room, meet each person where they are. Ask, what is comfortable for the audience in this moment given the circumstance. If you're communicating to a closed style, observe their body language, give them the desired space. Are they open to communicate at this time?

You may need to alter your preferred style to email and ask questions about systems. If the individual resembles the blind style, encourage them to express their knowledge and listen. If the person shows the hidden style, discern the amount of disclosure, and inquire questions to build trust.

Comprehending others, how they approach time and use words builds connection. One of my mentors prefers emails and quick phone calls, while I'm inclined to meet in person. To best connect, our phone calls are short and emails concise. Contrast with my client who lives two hours away and prefers in-person sessions, not efficient, but effective to see, hear, and feel body language.

Our communication style affects how we use words and feel about the moment. Prior to communicating, ask: Are you wanting to be there? Is it new in a healthy, professional way or a nerve-racking, hard, crucial conversation type of way? The best leaders are flexible when presenting their message. They adjust to what the audience and space need. In one day, I present the power of story to two different networking groups. One group has four people in attendance. The other twelve. When an audience is smaller, less formal, I present seated and facilitate as a casual conversation. In contrast, the second group responds well to standing and presenting the information. Consider your audience, the space, and the message for how you communicate.

Additionally, virtual communication requires adapting how we present information to connect with others. Whether it's a formal presentation or one-on-one conversation, magnetic speakers consider the style of their virtual backdrop (i.e., white board, bookshelf, or logo), bright lighting, clear, amplified sound with an external microphone, and overall professional presence. What you wear, how much of your body you show, the camera angle, gestures, and eye contact into the camera all are seen on a small, square screen.

During a past virtual networking call, an individual greeted me wearing pajamas in bed—obviously too casual. These choices hurt my first impression and influence a desire to jump off the call. I've dressed in what a friend calls "the business mullet," wearing professional attire on top and casual on bottom. This style affects my communication: I feel I'm not fully committed to the conversation or presentation. Instead, now, I dress head to toe professionally. To increase your audience's trust online, adapt: dress in your brand, stand when you speak, and display hand gestures on camera. Modify your space and note virtual communication demands more time and effort.

My client, owner and CEO of a family business, Heather, expounds on the importance of stretching her one-on-one preferred communication style during large monthly team safety meetings. She says, "Doing new, having fun, and referencing inside jokes keeps them [team] on their toes. I change it up and involve five to six people." While being her authentic self is important, identifying her communication style, what's natural, needs stretched and practiced. Her care for her team and the awareness of attracting their attention require altering her preferred style.

Change management expert Amber Howard explains how her communication style affects the audience engagement.

Howard moved to Bali in a leadership role and has been in the process of learning a new culture and language. She says, "I feed the audience energy, and as a result, they are enlivened. By using plain language, having a clear intention, and considering the audience's wants and needs, I can engage my audience. I manage my energy and the dimensions of my well-being." Communication style requires understanding our use of language and energy: what it is, how you acquire it, and how you give it away to others.

Magnetic speakers adapt.

* * *

LIMIT COMMUNICATION DISTRACTIONS
TO KEEP YOUR AUDIENCE ENGAGED

Your communication choices and style draw your audience in or distract them from your message. In an interview, speaker trainer Brian Drury defines the term "unconscious dissonance" to refer to anything a speaker does or says to pull the audience away from the journey the speaker is taking them on, interrupts the story flow, or elicits the wrong emotional response.

Drury lists seven examples of unconscious dissonance.

Speaking in absolutes

"The only way to…" or "This is absolutely true…"

Example: "The only way to lose weight is through the ketogenic diet."

The audience disengages knowing this statement is not always true (even if it is sometimes). Speakers have the responsibility of buffing these edges out.

Alternative: "For me and my clients, what has worked best…"

Plot holes or missing information

Link your stories together to create flow. Avoid plot holes unless you want a deliberate gap to create suspense or tension. By the end of the speech, "resolve the mystery." Use effective outlining to account for all key story elements. Practice for feedback.

From feedback, Drury changes the following statement in his keynote speech, "You never know whose life you'll change to be at your best," to "You'll never know whose life you'll change by choosing to act," which creates a clearer takeaway and response.

Overwhelming the conscious mind with too many facts and figures

"Out of the forty-nine million people surveyed, 23 percent found they had less results and out of those 23 percent, 17 percent had an exceptional result…" Have two to three deliberately selected statistics to enhance your message. The audience will remember key points and act on them.

Minimizing the audience's lived experiences

When you say, "I know exactly how you feel," this minimizes the uniqueness of the audience's pain and experience.

Additionally, it takes the focus off them and their struggle and puts it on the speaker. The focus should be entirely on the person sharing, giving them value and the story relevance.

Alternatives:

"I can't imagine what that was like for you."

"That must have been a huge challenge to get through. How are you feeling now after that experience?"

Unregulated emotional intensity

Honor the time and attention your audience gives you (two of their most valuable resources). Build a rapport and appropriate tone for the given context. Being too intense, too big, loud, or too quiet immediately from the start can be off-putting or cause the audience to disengage. Meet them where they are, and guide them through the message.

Environmental distractions

Anything on screen or stage can draw the audience's attention away or disrupt the flow of your presentation.

On-Stage: Doors opening or closing, phones ringing, slides not working.

Virtual/On-Screen: Cars driving by in the background or people walking past.

Lack of familiarity with the content

Filler words or phrases (i.e., "You know," "Um," "Ah," "Like," etc.)

Nervous motions like looking down or away, or movement like pacing back and forth on stage

Repetitive gestures

Repetitive words/phrases—Only repeat key words and phrases deliberately to persuade or emphasize a point.

* * *

Magnetism requires identifying your communication style and preferences, then recognizing other's preferred style may vary from yours. Audience-centeredness heightens when hearing what's actually being said and responding appropriately in the moment.

EXERCISE

Spend a day listening and observing. Take note of what communication style is your preference. How do others react to you in the workplace? Write down the verbal and nonverbal feedback and amount of self-disclosure you see and hear in different communications with people. What did you do well? What can be improved for next time?

REFLECTION QUESTIONS

What is my preferred communication style?

Where do I get my energy from (other people or inward reflection)?

When do I transition into a different communication style?

What have I noticed with others' communication style and preferences? How can I meet them where they are?

How can I advocate for what I need to communicate in my preferred style magnetically?

Have I presented any cognitive dissonance examples in previous talks? How would I change for the future?

PART II

YOUR MAGNETIC MESSAGE

PASSION LEADS TO A MAGNETIC MESSAGE

Let the passion for the subject become more powerful than the fear. Own that you have a bigger message, that you're the ambassador, not taking people's reactions personally.

—SHELLEY RIUTTA, PSYCHOTHERAPIST

Experienced product manager and Gallup Certified Strengths Coach Elvira Marie Chang crosses the dark, high school auditorium stage. As she approaches the microphone, she senses her nerves taking over. This moment from twenty-five years ago feels like yesterday to her now as she describes it.

Chang, a striking, spiritual, Chinese Cuban American woman embodies calm strength as she continues her story. In the late 1990s, as the boom to encourage women to pursue STEM careers spreads, Chang explains a high school principal contacts her engineering department and requests she speak. Unusual for her, she doesn't prepare for this speech. She simply arrives and speaks. "I still remember, it's like something came through me. I lost myself in the words and connected with the audience. Truly in flow."

I ask, "Why do you think you experienced such a powerful speaker flow?"

"For me, this speaking event came down to problem-solving. I didn't show up trying to persuade young ladies to pursue the engineering field or even promote engineering as a career. With the auditorium full of around one hundred young teenage women, I focused on one priority: How can I relate to this specific audience? How do I describe 'engineering' in terms that these young women can relate to and be interested in?"

As Chang shares her story, I inquire, "How did you know your talk landed with the audience?"

"It was more than how I felt about the topic. It was the engagement and feedback I received from the audience. Following my talk, students asked me questions, wanting to know more." Chang feels passion for her topic and connects the topic to her audience.

The *Webster Dictionary* defines *passion* as a strong emotion, having an overpowering or compelling effect; intense emotional drive or excitement; strong love or affection, fondness, enthusiasm for anything (1988). Generally, we think passion is for a person, however, passion can be toward an idea or speaking topic.

Curious to learn more about Chang's perspective on understanding the self, our strengths, and talents as a speaker, and aligning them to the passion of a topic, I probe further. "How did you apply the CliftonStrengths assessment during this talk to be magnetic?"

Chang notes CliftonStrengths helps people discover and describe their most common talents. She says, "Interestingly, 'communication' is not one of my top ten, even top twenty CliftonStrengths, yet I was able to connect with this audience. I used my relator, responsibility, connector, and adaptability talents." CliftonStrengths defines *relator as* naturally genuine and authentic; *responsibility* takes ownership of what we say and do; *connectedness* understands we're part of something bigger than ourselves; and *adaptability* is a here-and-now person, willing to respond to what the moment holds (Clifton and Rath 2017, 45-145).

Chang continues, "This speaking experience reminded me that ultimately being magnetic is about connection. For that to happen, we must be more connected with ourselves first, aligning with who we are, then connect our love of the topic with our audience."

Through our conversation, I'm reminded our passion for the subject is imperative to being magnetic. Chang discusses her value and the importance of letting communication organically evolve in each speaking engagement. While some individuals find it more natural to communicate, be more articulate and engaging, Chang emphasizes all of us have the capacity to mature a magnetic speaking talent in our own individualized way.

HOW DO YOU PASSIONATELY COMMUNICATE?

Love, really love what you do. Author Elizabeth Gilbert says, "All love becomes help" (Forleo 2015). Gilbert's writing earns rejection letters for years yet love and helping others push her to continue to write and speak. Change management expert and thought-leader Amber Howard explains, "Most people are not speaking to what they want. Are you creating what you want with your speaking?" Speakers need to explore what they care about, how they feel about their message, and put their hearts into their message for their desired outcome. Howard discusses the importance of our personal awareness, understanding we perceive the world differently than others. From understanding the self, Howard says, "Now add your obsession/passion, plus your emotions and feelings for your audience, along with story that communicates your passions and ideas." She ends, "A magnetic speaker is an expert in listening."

Listen to your heart. Listen to your audience. Listen and feel the passionate drive to move the conversation forward.

Research your audience.

Following a leadership workshop with healthcare professionals, a doctor steps forward and asks me, "How do you do it? How do you engage an audience in that way? Looking at each of us and drawing us in to your message?"

When I flashback to my four-hour communication presentation, I consider my temperament and topic. What do I value and care about? I value authenticity, having others view me as me, and I see others for who they are. My love of sharing communication style and supporting others motivates me to learn and share more. Prior to this presentation, I transform into Nancy Drew, a sleuth on a mission to learn all I can about my topic and how to land it with this healthcare audience. I'm not a medical professional, yet I have a mother and sister who are nurses. I talk with them and request information: What are the current medical trends and issues? What's important for healthcare professionals to hear? What do you feel they need to know to lead and communicate more effectively?

I connect with the specific medical institution and analyze their mission, vision, and current state of leadership and morale. I quote medical journals and note the importance of communication, including examples of overcoming failures. Finally, I create realistic role-plays to show versus tell.

Passionate speakers care for the specific audience. Because I value unique identity and authenticity, I work harder to incorporate this sentiment in my communication. Other speakers may have dissimilar values and go about preparing and presenting differently. Self-awareness and audience-centeredness affirm connection. Your passion inspires preparation and delivery, and audiences feel this magnetic, passionate energy. Work the topic into your heart first then massage the message into the hearts of your audience.

Be aware of meaningful topics.

Exploring meaningful topics grounds the speaker into the subject matter and connects more with the self and moment. Speakers can establish credibility based on their authority of the topic and their energy. If you want to be known as an expert in your field, present passionately. Author and

speaker Anne Lamott keenly writes and speaks about alco-
holism, motherhood, and Jesus unapologetically, with ruth-
less honesty.

Following my leadership workshop, enthusiasm for learning,
intuitive nature, and overall preoccupation with harmony and
passion for the subject matter influence my presentation style.
It's unique to me. My zeal for exploring what's possible (in this
case, growing heart-centered leadership in healthcare) and
peppering my talk with stories and analogies to demonstrate
"the how," enhances the workshop's delivery.

COMMUNICATE ONE PASSION, ONE SKILL.

Gary Keller highlights the importance of focusing on one
thing, and success in business comes from living your funda-
mental truth (2012, 117). Translate this mantra into speaking.
If you believe in what you say, one clear theme, your audience
will too. Author Bo Lozoff highlights living a life by having
a spiritual practice, living simply, and being of service (1999,
3). You can follow this same passionate philosophy when
you speak.

Tina's Tips to a Passionate Topic and Style:

First, acknowledge who you are. Honoring yourself affects
how you craft your passionate message and show up in
the world.

Second, the message needs to be simple. As authors Chip and
Dan Heath state, it's easier to be complex than simple (2008,
55-57). The heart's expression is simple.

Third, your words have power. Come into the communication with the goal to serve others. This makes your message more effective and long-lasting.

Embrace the spiritual being you are, your personality and talents.

Incorporate simplicity in the mechanics of your message and style. This includes preparation, speaker ritual, and vocal and physical delivery.

Integrate heart-centered service, being audience-centered with your message.

Spirit + Simplicity + Service = Passionate connection and impactful message.

THE TOPIC MATTERS TO ME

Dr. Kim Hoogeveen describes a previous speaking event, a signature talk title he's super passionate about. The topic structure matches his presentation title: "Stupid Things Leaders Do." This is his first time presenting this talk to 200 people. Dr. Hoogeveen says, "Those ninety minutes flew by due to *passion*, which seems to accelerate time. If you combine preparation and passion, matching title, topic, and approach with your personality style, the odds are high your audience will find it interesting. The 'Stupid Things' structure lent itself to more dark humor I naturally enjoy and made the speech more compelling than I could have made it using a 'Smart Things Leaders Do' approach. As a result, the presentation was fun, had a natural flow, and got a great reception—even a slightly embarrassing standing ovation."

Professor Gretta Berghammer says, "It matters to me. What I'm sharing, [the topic] matters to me. What do I want the audience to know and do with the content of my message? That's my point of entry. I can invite you [the audience] into what matters to me, but I can't force it upon you."

Berghammer and I discuss the mistake of defining passion as energy. Passionate feelings may involve intense love or hate emotions, whereas, passionate style doesn't have to display exuberant, large gestures, and a booming voice. A speaker may be over the moon about the idea and express it softly. Energy is physical and can be loud, whereas, passion is internal, and the idea matters to the speaker.

My spouse Lyle expresses soil health as his north star. He talks about it to advocate change. Each time he speaks from the heart. I've seen professionals who have never asked: Does my topic matter to me? Magnetic speakers impart themselves to their audience to make them part of the vision and solution.

Communication Studies Professor Dr. Marty Birkholt explains the importance of mindset to be magnetic. Magnetic speakers must truly feel the genuine, sincere passion for their topic, so the audience feels it. In his classroom, following disengaged student performances, the class has a follow-up discussion about how they clearly weren't excited about the leadership topic. Dr. Birkholt says, "If you're [the speaker] not in the game, then your audience will not be in the game. If your nonverbal communication contradicts your verbal message, it's like your subconscious is undermining, expressing 'this is unimportant, uninteresting.'"

His philosophy teaches students how to connect their emotional experience with their topic, and then authentically share it in a meaningful way. He reiterates, "Your mindset determines if your message is successful. You can't fake it [passion]." Passion truly comes from within.

Speaking with passion is true to your nature and love for the topic.

DISCOVER YOUR PASSION
If You Feel Stuck, Go Back to Childhood.

Comedian and keynote speaker Frank King tells his first joke in fourth grade. King blends his love, passion, and talent for comedy with mental health to make an impact. He says, "Be vulnerable on stage and expose all warts. Move them emotionally." Being funny about tough things comes naturally to him. In King's multiple TEDx Talks, he exhibits raw emotion and witty humor inspired by his childhood interest. He explores what's natural and fun as a child, which translates into a successful speaking career.

Take a Speaker Inventory.

Communication researchers Steve Duck and David McMahan explain the importance of taking an individual speaker inventory, developing a list of your knowledge, experiences, what you value, even likes and dislikes (2009, 304-305). This inventory becomes a starting part to craft your message. A speaker's inventory provides strategy and clarity with your communication. From your list, you can discover a potential hidden gem.

Align Your Message to Match Your Style.

Communication expert Stephen Lucas highlights selecting a speaking topic requires the topic be appropriate for the speaker and in alignment with the individual's speaker style. Lucas emphasizes, "Do not try to 'become' someone else when you speak" (2012, 18). Instead, select the ideas matching your speaker style and use of language. While I love to use humor in my presentations, I cannot imitate Jerry Seinfeld or Ellen DeGeneres who've mastered timing and dramatic pause in their delivery style.

Make the Topic Worthy of Your Audience's Time.

Ultimately, speaking passionately about a topic needs to be important to the speaker and worthy of the audience's time (Zarefsky 2011, 121-122). I've evolved my topics, stories, and examples to be relevant and timely, including coping with change and navigating uncertainty using the powerful tool of improvisation. All topics were in response to the pandemic.

Passion + Expertise + Usefulness = Magnetic Connection

Both clients and TEDx speakers Meg and Seth have created powerful talks by having a rich clarity and passion. For Meg, it's developing a nonprofit, Camp You-Can, and for Seth, soil health. Their enthusiasm for the topic pushes them to believe and know they can present a powerful talk. Declaring passion motivates message inspiration.

Passion is abstract; it's feeling the beautiful energy from the heart.

Passion is a belief in what you're saying.

Passion is a connection to your idea and audience.

Passion is expressed in your words, voice, and body.

Holistic psychotherapist Shelley Riutta says in a coaching call, "It's all about the alignment of the soul rather than a performance; cultivate the inside of you and the outside will follow." Riutta inspires me to explore specific dimensions to master the art of public speaking and subject matter. To be an effective speaker, find inner alignment, embrace your magnetism, explore your passion topic(s), and love of audience, and then be fully present. Through client work and research in the field of communication, I've created five dimensions to master the art of magnetic communication.

Tina's Five Dimensions to Master Magnetic Communication

Dimension 1: Mastery of Speaking: A Balanced Heart

To be a magnetic speaker, you need to channel your soul: balance your heart and head. Feel joy, not fear.

Dimension 2: Mastery of Speaking: Self-Love

To be a magnetic speaker, experience and embody self-love. Monitor where you are: the conditioned self or authentic self. Label and be the loving, wise adult.

Dimension 3: Mastery of Speaking: Audience-Centeredness

To be a magnetic speaker, know your audience, engage them with a variety of strategies, use different learning styles: audible, visual, kinesthetic, and written.

Dimension 4: Mastery of Speaking: Engaging, Organized Content

To be a magnetic speaker, embrace and communicate clear, engaging content. Keep your audience in the know.

Dimension 5: Mastery of Speaking: Anchored Confidence

To be a magnetic speaker, anchor in your confidence, overall presence, commit to your vision, and share your message for the greater good.

EXERCISE

Explore your passions. What did you love as a child? Find your passion topic. Look for your inner motivation then express it externally. What and how you say a message can move the conversation forward or kill it. List speaking topics you know and care about. What do you know how to do? What subjects are you currently reading about? What are you learning?

REFLECTION QUESTIONS

What experiences and people have affected and influenced me? Enhanced my passion or squelched it?

Energy comes from within the heart. What is important to my heart?

What am I curious about?

What can I investigate more?

Who would I like to share my passion with? What context or speaking space do I envision sharing my passion?

How can I show passion with my words, style, voice, body?

THE WHO THAT WE SHARE: WE'RE ALL STORYTELLERS

Always teach by story, because stories lodge deep in the heart.
—KENT NERBURN, AUTHOR OF "NEITHER WOLF NOR DOG"

At the heart of leadership lies persuasion. At the heart of persuasion lies storytelling.
—ESTHER CHOY, PRESIDENT OF LEADERSHIP STORY LAB

Everyone is a storyteller.

This is one of life's truths, yet, at one point, I failed to believe this statement. Over time, I've compared myself to other great storytellers, including my naturally charismatic and funny uncle, Don. Uncle Don brings to life the human experience through his adventurous escapades from asking a woman on a date and forgetting his wallet, to attending the wrong funeral visitation, to nearly meeting Elvis Presley when stationed in the army. Somehow, my uncle endears his audience into past moments and capitalizes on the rich sensory details of bumpy car rides on narrow European roads, to honest reactions and dialogue with various people, to the realness of the human experience.

Uncle Don is a talented storyteller; one I've aspired to be. A client prompts me to admit I am a storyteller and own it. Acknowledging this truth is significant to achieve success. Internal, negative mindsets affect what you say and how you say it. If a speaker questions their ability, their lack of self-confidence shines through words and body language and hurts potential impact. Belief, the inner knowing, and charged emotions connect the audience to the message.

"A story doesn't have to be a major life achievement like climbing Kilimanjaro to be important," says psychotherapist, writer/performer Jude Treder-Wolff. She suggests you don't have to climb Mount Kilimanjaro to share a powerful story. A story can emerge from something as simple as losing your car in a parking lot. Perhaps you've learned more about yourself or the kindness of strangers. It's stepping back and reflecting on the moment as it unfolds and then expressing the life lesson, what it means to be human. You don't need an Elvis to enter your story for it to be spectacular and move people to think differently or act.

To be a storyteller requires two components:

Own you are a storyteller; believe it. Show it.

Find the right story to make the desired impact.

BELIEVE YOU'RE A STORYTELLER

In 2009, at the end of my nearly nine-month pregnancy, I lost a child, my stillborn daughter Shirley Mae. Initially, I didn't think an audience wanted to hear about this experience. I worried about describing the ache and hurt. With a storytelling coach's encouragement, I crafted and performed the story on a New York stage. From this process, I learned more about my spouse's pain. Through this story, I discovered through loss, it's about moving forward, not moving on (Bakehouse 2016). Following this performance, a mother said, "Your story moved me. I too lost a child." My story became her story and the audience's story. Performing in front of a live audience helps others process their painful past experiences, provides healing, and evolves into a deeper connection as we journey together.

Even with a theatre degree and years of teaching communication, using the label "storyteller" has been challenging for me. I've asked these three questions:

Do I have the ability to connect deeply with an audience?

Do I have something worthy to share?

Will people care enough to listen?

Feeling the fear of boring an audience, a client says, "Haven't audiences heard too many stories about this topic?" I point out the differentiator is the storyteller. No one has had your exact experience. Audiences love to join the journey of something familiar with a fresh angle and viewpoint.

We empathize, feel, and embrace the storyteller's personal perspective. Author Chenjerai Kumanyika writes about crafting a story for *The Moth*, an international storytelling show and podcast. He expresses his challenge of viewing himself as a storyteller. *The Moth* encourages taking himself seriously. Kumanyika says, "You have important stories to tell. They are stories that no one else can tell. But you have to be willing to do the work of developing them—and then work through your fears to share them" (Bowles et al. 2022, xxii).

Unfortunately, we fail to believe we're storytellers. We hold the word "storyteller" up high as only a performative talent. We can embody what communication strategist John Capecci says in a past conversation, "We're all orators of our own lives." Once we invest in self-awareness, discover our story, we then allow it to flow from the heart.

I am a storyteller.

EMBRACE A STORYTELLING MINDSET

Personal stories reveal our inner lives, and sharing our vulnerability is daring and requires bravery. When you disclose personal information, release the profound fear you feel, it unleashes your potential. Storytellers embrace what speaker and consultant Anthony Sanni calls three storytelling mindsets: social, performance, and vulnerability (2023). The *social mindset* focuses on inclusivity, transforming the story from being "mine" to ours, involving the audience in the process. The *performance mindset* highlights the importance of style with your voice and body to draw an audience into the experience. The *vulnerability mindset* refers to the commitment to sharing your truth and your willingness to open up. Balancing these three mindsets and expressing your truth takes the audience through your point of view. It's finding the courage to step up and speak.

During a teen storytelling show, I witness high schooler Ali's voice shake and her eyes well up with tears as she explains how her dad struggles with drugs and alcohol and fails to believe in her. She learns she has to believe in herself to become the doctor she aspires to be. Her inner faith inspires the teen audience to their feet, the auditorium echoing in rich, vibrant applause.

After the show, a teen audience member asks Ali if she can take a picture with her. Ali asks, "Why?"

The teen responds, "I loved your story, and I struggle sometimes. So, when I feel down or am struggling, I'll reach for this picture for inspiration."

This teen storyteller leans into her fear, owns, and performs her truth. Her vulnerability impacts the audience. Know your story is valid, share your truth, and feel the emotions you feel. The audience's love for you will grow. First believe you can tell a story. Experience the energy when you share a story, trust, and own the mindset, that yes, you are a storyteller.

Awaken your inner storyteller. Pause. Let go of the fear. Share.

HOW DO YOU SELECT THE RIGHT STORY?

Finding Your Story

Label issues, themes, and events you're proud of or challenged by.
Explore family, friends, and work experiences.
Mine through firsts and failures.
Share your lessons learned.

Author Meg Bowles says, "I always say to think back to moments in your life that really shifted you in some way. Dig into that. When you think of a moment, ask yourself, 'Why did that moment stick with me? What about that moment was important to me?' You start to see patterns of your story arise... big decisions are a good place to find stories; so are embarrassing moments and mistakes. Think of a time you did something, but it didn't go as planned. Within these kinds of prompts you can begin to explore moments of vulnerability. Sometimes you have to figure out who you're not before you can become who you are. It's about being on the wrong path in life, having the courage to try things, and figuring out where our strengths really lie" (2022, 4).

"Pick a lane," Frank King, comedian and keynote speaker, says. King avoids being a commodity speaking expert. Instead, he selects one topic to talk about: suicide prevention. He emphasizes the importance of speaking from your heart, not your head.

Your life is interesting. Reveal your experience. It doesn't require a major accident, loss, or championship. Lessons learned matter. Your story helps others grow in their own personal journey of being human. Author and creator of organizational learning experiences David Hutchens says to ask yourself if you're telling the right stories, clarify your intent, engage, connect, and move people (2015, 76).

Ask questions.

Publisher and Creativity Doula, Hollis Citron helps people birth their ideas into the world. I ask, "How do you encourage others to tell stories?"

Upbeat and inspired, Citron says, "I was facilitating a clay-making workshop and opened with this question: 'Has anyone been told they weren't good at art?' Several hands shoot up. One man said his middle school art teacher broke every ceramic piece. I say, 'I hear that. That's frustrating.' Participants got an opportunity to emote and then we created art together."

I respond, "It's clear you created a space for them to speak."

She says, "They felt safe and wanted to be heard." When Citron asks an open-ended question, she initiates and encourages stories. Specific, guided questions focus and pull emotional memories from our past to inspire story.

Why Is It Challenging for Us to Share a Story?

Clients have mentioned two challenges: identifying a good story and crafting the story with a clear structure. Effective storytellers explore what problem they're trying to solve, ask why they're telling the story, and then investigate the best strategy to reach their outcome. Additionally, author Roy Peter Clark names three questions to ask:

"What's the point of the story?

Why are you telling the story?

What does your story say about life, the world, and the times we're in" (2006, 150-153)?

From these questions, break your story into three acts: Act I sets the scene, creates context. Act II takes the audience on your journey, engaging in internal or external conflict. Act III resolves the conflict, sharing the complete lesson learned.

Storytellers provide context, conflict, and complete the message with personal transformation.

WHAT DO STORIES NEED?

Stories need an audience.

During a past high school class, students reinforced a significant storytelling concept. I asked: "What does a story need?" I expected answers to range from characters, plot, conflict, to setting. Surprisingly, a student spoke up and said, "Don't all stories need an audience?"

Why yes! If you're sharing a story and an audience isn't present or choosing to listen to you, then did the story happen? To gain trust with your audience, care. Guide your stories with the following questions:

What do you want your audience to know?

What do you want your audience to feel?

What do you want your audience to do?

Stories need an objective.

My nonprofit client decides storytelling will increase potential partnerships and fund a future project. I coach them to share testimonials of personal growth. The act of hearing individual improvement intensifies emotional responses from their audience, and later, attracts funders to their building project. Each of them practice sharing their stories in conversation, which empowers them and clarifies and strengthens their message.

Darcy Maulsby, Iowa storyteller and marketer, explains no one can copy your story. You put your own stamp on it. She says, "Be strategic in filing stories ready to share in your back pocket. Ask yourself, 'What do I have to offer that can benefit the audience's life?'"

Stories come in handy in other circumstances. I've used stories to attract potential clients, connect at networking events, or entertain at parties. Be clear on the story's purpose and how it benefits listeners. Your story serves others. What do you want the story to do for you? Think with the end in mind.

Stories need emotional truths.

Comedian and keynote speaker, Frank King, says in his TEDx Talk, "I suffer from depression and have thought about killing myself more times than I can count… This dark passenger has tried to kill me multiple times. I came very close in 2010" (King 2017). With 80 percent of his speaking business gone and having to file for bankruptcy, King continues his story. He has an itch: to use his nickel-plated thirty-eight to take his life. Three words prevent him from doing it: "My wife Wendy."

Through his heartfelt, honest story, he explains great copy isn't as powerful as a mediocre story with vulnerability. He emphasizes, "I'm not a psychologist, but I can tell you how the barrel of my gun tastes like. My truth? I tasted relief" (King 2017). King displays powerful, raw emotion and a willingness to stand firmly in his painful truth. Know your style is your own and what you think and how you feel about your experience is your truth, no one else's.

WHY TELL STORIES?

During a 2019 Applied Improvisation Conference, I'm fifteen feet away from Alan Alda, and I'm freaking out. I've always been a huge fan of his ever since he performed in the television series *M*A*S*H* then *The West Wing,* and now more than ever as he trains scientists to communicate their ideas effectively using the powerful tool of improvisation. You can imagine my surprise when he asks for a volunteer to join him on stage.

Enthusiasm sparks up inside. Our eyes lock. He slowly raises his arm in my direction and gestures to the woman sitting directly in front of me. The eager volunteer runs to the stage. Alda gives her this directive: "Take this glass half full of water and walk across the stage." She strolls to the end of the stage with ease.

Alda fills the glass full and hands it to her, saying: "Take this full glass of water and walk across the stage without dropping a single drop, or your whole village will die." The audience gasps as she progresses purposefully to the other end of the stage. We chant, "You go, you got this, you go girl!" Once she places the full glass of water on the coffee table, we all erupt excited cheers. Our whole village didn't die! Alda steps forward and says, "Now that's the power of a great story. It has high stakes; it's a shared experience, and it connects us." Alda stresses what I already know: the power of story. Stories make a message more magnetic.

Our brains react to story.

We're wired for story. It's in our nature to listen and share stories, for they provide a pattern to stimulating experiences, exploring and explaining social norms, rules, reactions, and feelings without the listener having to "pay the full cost" (Bhalla 2013). Our brains react to story and motivate us to act. Through multiple studies, Paul Zak's lab discovers the neurochemical oxytocin is produced when a participant hears character-driven stories (Zak 2014). Furthermore, Zak finds the amount of oxytocin the brain releases predicts "how much people are willing to help others" (2014). Nonprofits can use story to persuade funding for projects and businesses for selling products and services.

Stories are more powerful than data.

In 1987, the world watches as baby Jessica falls in her aunt's eight-inch well. The media's coverage moves my child self to ponder, "What if this happened to me?" whereas my parents think, "What if that happened to our daughter?" Compare this specific example to saying, "One out of twenty children fall in a well each year." Audiences care less about the general (expressed in data) and more about the specific individual (shared through story).

Stories having healing power.

Annie Brewster MD explains on her blog, storytelling helps people reflect and edit the experience as our lives evolve and is part of the healing process (2021). Brewster uses story to cope with her multiple sclerosis diagnosis and states, "By sharing and receiving stories, we can help ourselves and others; we can build and strengthen relationships; we can move closer to self-acceptance and self-love" (Brewster 2021). Your pain expressed through story enables people to construct meaning from devastating events and begin to repair the hurt of their experience.

During an interview, Jude Treder-Wolff cites philosopher Søren Kierkegaard, "Life can only be understood backward, but it must be lived forward." We discuss storytelling affirms understanding our lives backward and gain perspective from exploring and conversing about our experiences in narrative form. Treder-Wolff explains our thoughts and feelings change over time as new information and insights come to us, impacts our identity, and our view of pain.

Stories illustrate a point.

Speakers need to be clear on the "why" of story to allow the audience to process and make the content relevant and relatable to their lives. My childhood friend Heather mentions reading a book containing too many stories (good stories, thoughtful stories), yet feels something is missing. The author leaves out processing the "why" and "how," which builds and shapes the curiosity to the "what." I agree with my friend: a story can illustrate a point, shape our perspective, help us know and do better, but if there's no application to know how to solve a problem or grow and stretch into a better human being then the story leaves a listener hanging. It's like hearing a powerful theory and having absolutely no idea how to apply it.

Stories enhance the speaker's likability.

As a powerful, persuasive tool, stories motivate an audience to buy into a project or idea. Working with a client, we discuss how the community can support a big, future project. I stress the importance of the marketing strategy to have the audience "know, like, and trust" the speaker. But, how can stories make you known? More likable? Trusted?

Start with a childhood story about yourself and relate to your topic. For example, if your project focuses on the arts and attracting more arts into your community, share a story of when you realized art was important to you, a first memory of doing or experiencing art, and share those sensory details, inner thoughts, and emotions. Personal stories humanize the speaker, especially examples from childhood, as they show vulnerability and the realness you are a person. As you build on your humanness, you're becoming more likable, essential to building rapport. The more likable you are, the more you gain listeners, feedback, and support. We are more apt to do what someone says or believes if we like them. Incorporating stories in your communication build, grow, and create community with your audience.

Stories establish and strengthen credibility.

Expand your likability and heighten credibility to include stories from current partners of the project. Have your partners reveal what they've done or what has happened in their work and align with your proposal. For example, if you're trying to establish more visible art in your community, have current partners disclose stories about the impact art has on their lives and why they've decided to participate in the project. The more you tap into their "why" and the more others see and hear the "why," the more apt support will grow. Stories from others build your likability and establish a stronger credibility for the idea. When others say art, mental health, agriculture, education, etc., are worthwhile, then your message will resonate more. Repetition strengthens your personal credibility and begins to convert belief systems and push for positive action.

Stories provide concrete hope.

By expressing the utopian vision of what can be, the possibilities and potential, you provide word pictures the audience concretely sees, feels, and starts to experience. It's one thing to say, "Art is important for our community to thrive," or "Support conservation." Most audiences agree, yes, art and conservation are important. Yet, they hesitate to financially support a vague project or abstract idea without clarity of what it is and the process steps.

To earn backing on your idea, address the "why" first, followed by the "what" and the "how," as Simon Sinek discusses in his TED talk (Sinek 2014). If a community wants to grow a STEM project, reveal researched, qualitative stories, which include data to back up STEM as a strong, well-planned, organized, and worthwhile program to improve your community. Add testimonials from similar projects to build on the hope, vision, and expansion to greater message impact.

True stories build trust.

Make your audience the hero in your story to strengthen trust. Have them picture themselves experiencing the project. Articulate emotional details of how outdoor art will make them feel when they walk through town, or the empowerment a student will feel with access to additional educational resources. Being part of something bigger, outside of ourselves, is empowering. Create three different potential characters to represent your target audience for the project. Ask yourself: Who will experience this project? How will they experience it? What do they look like? Act like? What's important to them? Create realistic characters based on actual community members.

For a new technology center in a rural community, it might look like this:

> Sixteen-year-old is interested in a part-time CNA job and needs training to support their dream of one day becoming a nurse.

Forty-plus-year-old wants to start a small business and leave corporate; needs training and support on finances and building a business proposal.

Sixty-five-year-old appreciates learning, personal growth, and desires professional development to support their volunteer projects.

By developing realistic community characters, your audience sees themselves in the story and feels the emotions to be part of something greater and bigger. Stories express our integrity, who we are as a person. Through stories, our imagination can touch hearts and build trust with our audience.

Why do we tell stories? Everyone has experiences, times when we've wanted to complain, celebrate, or explore a new, exciting development. As Alda reminds us, stories create a shared experience, connects us, and can do good in the world. Let the story do the work.

EXERCISES

Explore past stories. What's my favorite childhood story and why?

When did I first share stories? What were my emotions and others' reactions to my story?

Mine for the gold. You have stories with every phase of life. Stories have stay power. Go for a nature walk with a notebook and pen. Set the intention to explore personal stories. Start with a guide word, an emotion, or theme. For example, "perseverance," "failure," "leadership," etc., can guide you on your storytelling journey. Or flow through your life chronologically: childhood to adulthood, personal to professional stories.

Create a storytelling file folder or journal, either electronic or hard copy. Continue gathering stories, yours and others', to illustrate points when you speak in presentations, meetings, or professional conversations.

Pay attention with a storyteller lens. For example, when attending a child's sporting event, observe, listen, notice more. What are you seeing? Feeling? Experiencing? Did an underdog team win a game? Explore the life lesson. By setting the objective of looking for story, you'll be surprised at how many stories come to life and shine through a normal, everyday event.

Use story to do the following: hook your audience into your keynote, open a team meeting, illustrate a point/idea in the body of your presentation, close a message to resonate.

Consume great stories: listen to *The Moth* podcast; attend a storytelling show; read nonfiction, fiction, and children's books. Take note of how you connect with the theme, plot, and characters.

Storytelling builds relationships with others. Practice in your day-to-day conversations with loved ones. Request their feedback.

REFLECTION QUESTIONS

Provide an example of a great storyteller from your family or friend group. What makes them effective? What interesting qualities do they possess?

Stories create meaning. What stories can I tell? What is the life lesson or meaning behind my story?

Why am I telling this story to this audience at this moment?

Where might I depart from my speaking outline to imbed a story or example to support my message?

PREPARE AN AUDIENCE-CENTERED MAGNETIC MESSAGE

———

Find a subject you care about.
Don't ramble, though.
Keep it simple.
Have the guts to cut.
Sound like yourself.
Don't be boring.

—KURT VONNEGUT, AUTHOR

"I have a fun, creative project for us," Grandma Shirley declares excitedly over the phone. I know I'm in for something interesting: Like the time we refinished an old table for a 4-H project, only to find no amount of sanding and dye will fix its dilapidated condition. Or the time we organized her upstairs closet, trying on 1950s prom dresses. Or the time we hand-washed thirty rugs in her ringer washer. My grandma finds pure pleasure in the simplicity of work for work's sake. She'd always say, "There's nothing better than a job well done and feel you were a part of it."

I respond, "Yes," and jump in my car for the one-hour trek to Grandma's farm with anticipation for our new project.

Adjusting her faded, floral-printed apron and removing her rubber gloves, Grandma creaks down the wooden stairs to her old, rustic farm basement filled with shelves of canned garden tomatoes and green beans lining the brick walls. Gram gestures to a brand-new Maytag washing machine and says, "I don't know how this thing works. Will you help me?"

Looking at her glistening, white washer up and down, I think, *I'm not a tech specialist, but this can't be too difficult.* "What's the problem, Gram?"

She replies, "I don't know how to start."

She complies a load of her chore clothes. Scanning the washer, I see she's twisted the dial to the desired selection. After glancing over the washer's facade, I tell her to turn the knob to "normal" and press "start."

Puzzled, she says, "That's it?"

"Yes, Gram. That's it. It's that easy."

We proceed to practice with a couple of loads to instill in Grandma the confidence to complete laundry on her own.

My grandma is used to her older way of washing laundry. She doesn't anticipate a task she's done for more than seventy years can be easier, simplified, and possible. My grandmother's expectation the process will be super complicated keeps her from being able to notice how simple it actually is to operate.

This limited belief and mindset prevents people from learning how to be magnetic speakers.

Magnetic speakers prepare and have a process.

MAGNETISM STARTS WITH AUDIENCE-CENTEREDNESS

Context leads to content. Assess the audience, speaking situation, and the desired outcome for each communicative event. Magnetic speakers aim for audience-centeredness, getting audiences to know, like, and trust the speaker. Additionally, speakers must let go of what Nancy Duarte calls "me-ness" (2023). Audience-centeredness happens when the speaker expresses experiences, common interests, and stories geared toward attracting audience attention. Release egocentrism and do what communication expert Stephen Lucas emphasizes as the speaker's responsibility: encourage audiences to choose to listen and take what the speaker says seriously (2012, 53).

Speaking and marketing coach Sarah Archer says, "Magnetic speakers absolutely craft content for an audience. It's putting the audience first." We discuss the importance of knowing the audience intimately as a speaker and connect with them where they are. With a background in stand-up comedy and theatre, Archer explains how a great talk should be like a dance between speaker and performer, each needing and feeding off the energy of the other. She emphasizes the importance of letting go once you've done the preparation, be present with your audience, and bring your whole self to deliver your message with passion and commitment. Archer stresses, "This [commitment] shifts your talk from awkward to awesome."

Client and politician Cole highlights the importance of audience-centeredness during his campaign for county recorder. He says, "When I announced my candidacy, people knew me, but it was my first time as a candidate to showcase my public speaking skills and make a good first impression with voters, tailoring my message as much as I can. I don't give the same speech in the same way to all different types of people." Cole sees the importance of customizing his content to different audiences to reach voters and make his desired impact.

Years ago, a church invited AgArts Executive Director and author Mary Swander to read a homily at a Catholic service on Good Friday. She shared her experience of preparing a traditional homily, which includes a story, illustration, and ends with Bible scriptures and prayer. Seated in a conference center, not a church, Swander noticed fully dressed nuns chanting, "Oh Mother Earth," praying for the earth's renewal. Quickly, she realized what she'd prepared wasn't appropriate for that audience and tone of service. Based on what she saw, heard, and felt, Swander created a talk focused on reverence for the land and soul, a more nontraditional meditation. Swander says, "I flexed my content to meet the needs of the audience. It's important to know your audience." Even in different contexts, both speakers embrace audience-centeredness to be more magnetic with their message.

KEEP YOUR AUDIENCE IN THE KNOW: SPEAK TO DIFFERENT LEARNING STYLES

Humor Engineer Andrew Tarvin discusses in an interview he creates keynote presentations with 75-80 percent as the same content and 20 percent customized with language and examples geared toward his specific audience. In addition to content choices, referring to your audience using the pronouns "we," "us," and "you," or naming the specific organization and providing distinct stories make the speaker more relatable. For example, saying, "As *sales managers, your* persuasive technique matters" identifies both your audience (sales managers) and communicates to them (your). Thus, this technique motivates audiences to choose to listen and remember the information.

Retaining messages requires true connection, speaking to auditory, visual, and kinesthetic learning styles.

Auditory learning style includes sharing story, humor, and varying vocal pitch, projection, and pause. Sir Ken Robinson's TED talk illustrates the importance of creativity and how it's diminished in schools through his rich sense of humor, powerful vocal pauses, and stories (Robinson 2007).

The visual learning style involves slides, video, props, and simple pictures. Bill Gates releases a swarm of mosquitoes in his TED talk to emphasize individuals in poor countries shouldn't be the only ones to have exposure to the deadly disease of malaria (Gates 2015). Additionally, during Jill Bolte Taylor's TED talk, she holds a human brain to highlight its functions and explain her experience of having a stroke (Bolte Taylor 2009). The use of visual aids enhances their messages.

Finally, kinesthetic learning style provides audience movement and participation. Here are examples of reaching your audience in a kinesthetic way:

Raise your hand if… or stand if…
Ask a rhetorical question: How many of you…?
Use a participant for a demonstration
Hold a prop
Engage audience in a pair share

AUDIENCE-CENTERED SPEAKERS
ORGANIZE THEIR MESSAGE

Author Roy Peter Clark highlights writing expert Donald Murray's stairstep to idea creation, which starts general, collecting ideas, and then focuses on one main idea, drafting, and finally revising (2006, 241). Magnetic speakers have a clear vision of their message. Through audience analysis, they start with what the audience knows then simplify the structure and wording for clarity. If speakers eliminate jargon, balance data, embed stories, and provide insightful information in digestible bites, audiences will comprehend and feel the message is for them.

Singer, keynote presenter, and coach Stephanie Bonte-Lebair explains what she calls balancing our three voices: purpose, mental, and physical voice. The *purpose voice* is what you mean to say and helps focus the intention of your talk. The *mental voice* includes the words to structure your talk. The *physical voice* aligns delivery with your purpose, context, and style.

When developing the body of your message, ask the following questions:

What does the audience know?
What does the audience need to know?
Why should the audience care about this message?

Speakers select and arrange their ideas to make sense for both the speaker and audience to recall the information (Zarefsky 2011, 210). Magnetic speakers do the following:

> State a clear purpose (inform—teach a concept, persuade—lead to an idea, motivate—move with emotions).

> Use a clear organizational pattern based on their purpose (chronological, topical, problem-solution, pros-cons, etc.).

> Start with a hook to pique the audience's interest in the topic (story, quote, startling fact, etc.)

> Close the message in a poignant way (story, utopian vision, challenge the audience, etc.)

In the body of your presentation, balance your main points. When attending a wedding, the bride is the focal point, followed by bridesmaids. The message's thesis becomes the bride, and the bridesmaids are the supportive main points. Magnetic speakers spend equal time on each main point, similar to one bridesmaid doesn't stand out from the others. Engage the audience. Include flare in the middle of the message. The second speaking point resembles middle child syndrome, feeling forgotten. Jazz up the middle with story, props, audience engagement, or repeat phrases, use longer pauses, and emphasize certain words.

Previewing signposts your point and keeps the audience in the know. When I present, I end every presentation's introduction with listing my three main points. For example, "In order to communicate effectively, you must first know yourself, second, know your communication context, and finally, know your audience." In Steve Jobs' 2005 Stanford commencement speech, Jobs previews he's going to share three stories. His strategy provides predictability and keeps the audience's thoughts with the speaker rather than on their distracting, inner self talk.

When you speak, sentence length and number of examples must match your intent. Use your words strategically.

"Use one example for power

Two for comparison, contrast

Three for completeness, wholeness, roundness

Four more to list, inventory, compile, expand"
(CLARK 2006, 98-102).

End strong. In former First Lady Michelle Obama's 2008 Democratic Convention speech, she strategically ends by providing personal references as "Mom and Chief," utopian vision for the "American Dream," and calls the audience to action, "vote for my husband Barack Obama." Finally, end with a poignant punch. Toward the end of former First Lady Barbara Bush's 1990 commencement address at Wellesley College she says, "And who knows? Somewhere out in this audience may even be someone who will one day follow in my footsteps and preside over the White House as the president's spouse, and I wish him well" (Quercus 2006, 182-183). This compelling line ends with rousing audience applause.

Tina's Tips to Prepare and Organize Your Talk

Start with the end in mind. How much time do you have? The shorter the speech, the less the amount of content. No amount of talking faster will move your message to the deadline.

Choose the best time of day to brainstorm. Identify your freshest, primary time to generate ideas and block out time to create.

Brainstorm on paper in a different setting (i.e., outdoors under a tree or by water). Rather than type, handwrite your ideas without judgment. Keep writing even if you don't feel like it. Let go of resistance in a new space to uncover fresh ideas. The more you write, the more ideas flow from your fingers.

Edit and cut more content than you think. The shorter the speech or story, the more preparation required. Select what's essential. Don't be married to your writing. Let go of the fluff and choose the meat.

Deliver your message extemporaneously.

Speaking and marketing coach Sarah Archer shares her experience in stand-up. "I was doing a gig, and the audience loved it. A promoter was in the audience and said to me, 'You did really good. You know what's stopping you? Your set feels fully scripted.' I realized I have to let go of the script and trust." Magnetic speakers devise a plan and speak extemporaneously from the heart.

Audience + Words + Feelings + Context = Audience-Centered

Crystal clear message + humanity = magnetism.

DEVELOP AN ENGAGING HOOK

Baseball player Lou Gehrig opens his speech, "Fans, for the past two weeks, you have been reading about a bad break I got. Yet today, I consider myself the luckiest man on the face of the earth" (Quercus 2006, 95-97). Known as the "Iron Horse" due to his durability, Gehrig holds back tears when addressing the crowd. His speech informs them of his forced retirement due to the deadly diagnosis of ALS. Gehrig uses the element of surprise, stating he's the "luckiest man on the face of the earth."

His honesty and humility hook the audience.

Magnetic speakers use atypical approaches to connect. Gehrig hooks with his reveal of the rawness and reality of leaving the sport he loves. Each time you speak, open with an attention-getter to resonate with your audience.

Potential hooks to start a talk or meeting:

Demonstrate an idea with prop(s)

Illustrate a point through story

Request the audience to participate

Ask a rhetorical question

Present a shocking fact

Share a thoughtful quote

Demonstrate a skill or surprise

Consider starting your speech in an uncommon way to pique interest. The audience has two options: *tune into* your message or *tune you out*. Make the hook easy on the listeners' ears. The less your audience works, the more they'll choose to listen.

MAGNETIC SPEAKERS SPEAK TO THE AUDIENCE'S PREFERENCES
Are You More Random or Sequential?

In conversation, I naturally jump topics. My patient spouse says calm and quietly, "Tina, I love your passion and enthusiasm. I need more clarity to follow your message. Would you consider using more transitions?" His compassionate question reminds me the importance of letting the audience know where I'm going with my message.

Speakers have distinct, preferred patterns and styles of communicating. I'm random. He's sequential. I let my passion lead what I say and how I say it. He follows facts and logic. When presenting, it's crucial to have clarity and a spicy style to create texture in your talks. Random communicators may express inner dialogue, jump from idea to idea, and work harder to formulate a sequential pattern. In contrast, the sequential communicator may question what details to eliminate and have too much content. Agendas are helpful for both styles to stay on track during meetings.

In a recipe, chefs mix ingredients in a certain way to create an outcome. Most muffin recipes mix dry ingredients then add liquid to the batter. A sequenced order of what ingredient goes first, second, and beyond, matters. Yet, random choices add flavor. Inserting fresh lemon zest to the batter boosts a tangy flare. Magnetic speakers organize their talk yet are willing to deviate from their specified pattern to clarify a point or relate more effectively with their audience.

When facilitating workshops, I clarify three, specific points in a sequenced manner and tailor the message to meet the needs of my audience. When an audience is confused, resists the content, or desires to dive in and invest more time, my random nature customizes examples. To empathize with my audience, I've used personal examples of when it was hard for me to speak on stage or imbed a humorous story of chasing Tom Selleck in a parking lot to engage. The goal is to check for understanding and identify gaps in content comprehension.

Clear Content and Intentional Order = Increased Understanding and Impact

Keep your audience in the know to have the influence you desire.

USE ABSTRACT ANALOGIES AND CONCRETE WORDS

People vary in speaking preferences, abstract concepts, or concrete terms. Idaho State University defines abstract words "refer to intangible qualities, ideas, and concepts, which indicate things we know only through our intellect, like 'truth,' 'honor,' and kindness.'" Concrete words are "tangible, qualities or characteristics, things we know through our senses like '102 degrees,' 'obese Siamese cat,' and 'deep spruce green'" (2016).

Abstract words = symbolic, theoretical, possibilities
Concrete words = specific, literal, factual, details

Dr. Kim Hoogeveen provides an example of concrete versus abstract language. He says, "Are you a good leader? And what exactly is 'leadership,' and what does it mean to be 'good?' Compare how challenging it is to answer this question: 'Are you able to run a mile under four minutes?'" The abstract concept "leadership" is difficult to objectively measure, thus individuals overestimate their leadership skills. In contrast, running a four-minute mile is a testable, concrete construct.

My client Heather, CEO of her family business and a motivated visionary and abstract communicator, struggles with explaining her company's growing mission to her team. "They just don't understand," she laments. The abstract idea of what's possible and why it's necessary to move forward makes sense to her but has left her sales team and others behind. They wrestle with the idea of change and worry about the uncertainty of attracting new and different clients.

Her desired expectations to improve, grow, and change quickly fail to answer the question her team needs to hear: "What's in it for me?"

We construct a verbal road map, an organized plan, to make her abstract idea more concrete:

Create a utopian vision hook. Lay out the ideal picture of what's to come. Align with who the organization is and where it's going.

Describe the current and future culture from a positive angle.

Invite feedback. Give the team a voice to be part of the change.

State the opportunity and list benefits for the decision.

Create a clear solution for the team's journey. Discuss the vision to strengthen positive feelings to navigate change.

My client applies inclusive language to keep her team in the conversation. Abstract communicators love utopian visions and dream of a world of possibility. What's essential, however, is including definitions of abstract terms, concrete examples, and clear benefits to justify the change. Finally, communicate your team as part of the solution with specific steps for what's next.

Conversely, balance concrete concepts with abstract language. Client, Lean Six Sigma expert, Tony, provides this strategy to secure healthcare process improvement. As a concrete communicator, he understands how to implement Lean Six Sigma. The challenge? Getting buy-in from his team.

As he teaches the process, he sees confusion and hears skepticism. We deliberate over the steps and why adopting Lean Six Sigma will be useful. He realizes explaining the process before expressing its importance hurts overall support for new procedures. His team needs to hear the abstract "why" to be persuaded first then proceed forward into the "how." His concrete preference with the "how" limits progress; however, once he balances the abstract and concrete communication style, he witnesses more questions with how to take small steps toward change. Soon, his team opens up to trying something new.

PROFESSIONAL EXAMPLE: EARNING A GRANT—*TOUCH THE MOON PROJECT*
Hook Your Audience to Listen. Create Passionate Tension

Theatre Professor Gretta Berghammer opens her presentation with these questions: "Did you ever as a kid look up at the stars and moon and wonder what it's like? Or thought about what it's like to see something new for the first time?" To build rapport with the audience, she shares her 1969 childhood moon-landing memory. Following her story, she asks, "Do you remember trying something completely new? How did you feel? What if I told you I created that moment of discovery for children?"

Berghammer's story gets the audience to feel and experience her past, persuading them to act. She recalls the moon landing touched her imagination. Her story illustrates Berghammer's passionate feelings about the "Touch the Moon" project and evokes a bond with the audience. At the core of communication is passion, a speaker-created tension.

Berghammer's Steps to an Audience-Centered Magnetic Presentation:

Share a clear vision of the project to earn funder support.

Talk to your target audience with energetic passion.

Brand the project's theme and move the audience into those feelings, inviting them into the dream.

Use supportive visuals to make the abstract idea more concrete.

Present the proposal. Open with a core curiosity question and deliver with enthusiasm: why I think this is so important, and why should you join me.

During the process, be open to modifying the theme and strategy based on the needs of the audience. Berghammer alters her theme to meet the timeliness of the fiftieth anniversary of landing on the moon. Additionally, she identifies a concrete problem in a creative way: immersing autistic children into a theatre experience.

Engage your audience instead of describing the possibilities: that's where the real power is.

* * *

Change management and thought leader Amber Howard explains audiences want to "feel gotten." Howard's Landmark Worldwide training defines "being gotten" as how we interpret our own experience of being in communicating with others. There's a technique to allow others to experience being seen. Howard says, "They're seen for exactly what they said, their experience, and what they're committed to, not what I perceive they are communicating." If we step into understanding the other, in a way that has them experience being gotten, then we can resolve any challenge.

Prepare an audience-centered message. Then, your audience will feel gotten.

EXERCISES

Select an upcoming keynote presentation, workshop, or team meeting. Audit it for audience-centeredness tactics.

Identify places where you can connect with the audible learner through story, the visual learner through props, pictures, or visual aid, the kinesthetic learner through movement, and the writing learner though reflection. Start with what's most natural to you, then weave in other speaking strategies to engage your audience to listen to your message.

Read frequently. Listen to speeches. Write daily, regular stories to build linguistic intelligence. Speak your ideas aloud and ask for feedback.

REFLECTION QUESTIONS

What does my audience care about? How can I relate and be relevant?

How do I prepare my talks? When is the best time of day for me to create?

What kinds of learning opportunities am I engaged in to build knowledge and content?

How will I start my message in an engaging way? Organize the body clearly? End poignantly?

What sources am I reading on the topic?

Am I more of a random or sequential communicator? Abstract or concrete?

How can I use concrete and abstract words and elements of random to enhance my communication? Is my communication balanced?

FOSTER CURIOSITY AND PLAYFUL CREATIVITY TO BE A MAGNETIC SPEAKER

———

*Creativity is seeing what others see and
thinking what no one else ever thought.*

—ALBERT EINSTEIN

Every day, during a Serengeti safari, South African Dr. John dons an Indiana Jones-style hat, khaki shorts, knee-length, white socks, and hiking boots, occupying the front seat of a jeep. A true erudite, Dr. John turns the lengthy jeep rides into rich tutorials on health, business, and life. I linger on his every word.

As we say our goodbyes, in a fog of sadness, tears stream down my face, and I ask, "What should I share with my college students?" Without hesitation, Dr. John replies with a soft sigh and soothing warmth, "Always be curious and always ask questions. That's never failed me in my fifty-plus years of practicing medicine." He explains curiosity reveals patient problems, and his medical success involves investigating and digging deeper. His steadfast curiosity creates positive relationships and enables his patients to connect and heal.

To improve at anything, we must be enticed with seeking knowledge and asking questions. Ciero defined curiosity as the "passion for knowing." Passion drives our desire to know and discuss our topic.

Curiosity is a choice. To improve communication, magnetic speakers commit to exploring and learning more and train their brains to inquire. Instead of jumping to conclusions, consider probing further. Engage in searching for answers to "why?" Stretch your curiosity by reading, listening, and attending events addressing topics from different points of view. Visit spaces as a student seeking new perspectives.

Magnetic speakers are curious.

CURIOSITY CONNECTS TO MAGNETIC COMMUNICATION

Magnetism derives from curiosity. When speakers personify a curious nature, it converts to contagious energy.

Curious speakers research their topic passionately.

Curious speakers experiment with different ideas.

Curious speakers continue to ask questions.

Grounded and enthusiastic explorers, magnetic speakers gain and maintain their audience's attention.

Be curious. Ask questions. Stand in your magnetism and speak.

CURIOSITY EMBRACES THE KNOWLEDGE GAP

Author Ian Leslie states curiosity is stimulated by understanding the absence of an existing gap of information (2015, 10). He claims our curiosity grows more intense when we recognize what we don't know. However, Leslie notes we're bad at identifying our information gaps. Curiosity holds an intellectual need to answer questions.

When a speaker provides interesting insights or a fresh perspective on a topic, this closes the gap of not knowing and delivers more clarity on a pattern with our previous knowledge. Thus, the audience's curiosity grows. During the October 2022 Women Lead Change Conference, keynote speaker and communication confidence coach Nada Lena Nasserdeen steps forward, upbeat and self-assured, and discloses her six pillars of confidence into clear, digestible nuggets. She offers four distinct strategies to be more confident, ranging from our belief system to backstory. Like Detective Sherlock Holmes hunts down clues and pieces them together to solve a mystery, Nasserdeen unravels the internal mystery of how to increase our confidence. She makes the abstract concept more concrete, thus, satisfying the audience's need to know that yes, this difficult question of how to be confident, can be answered.

MAGNETIC SPEAKERS SOLVE CONCEPTUAL MYSTERIES

"Mysteries arise from our attempts to understand and explain the world and our lives. Thus, they are products of our inquiring into what is real. The sense of philosophical mystery is an intellectual reaction to what we do not know" (Jones 2018, 2). Through speaker's stories, audiences explore mysteries to overcome failure, perseverance, or understand the identity of self. Mystery in stories leads to hearing new insights and posing potential solutions to problems. In story, an audience wonders what will happen next in the plot or the lesson learned. As we listen, we want to solve the ending to the story.

During Nasserdeen's same 2022 keynote, her story of starting her business (something new) addresses the "what" and "how." She provides action steps of managing her beliefs, making the time, being a content activator, and surrounding herself with an energized, supportive council. Nasserdeen answers the question: "Are you making the time to do the work and skills?" Her story expands throughout the talk and chips away at closing the information gap.

Nasserdeen's examples and story intrigue the audience. The balance of information establishes her credibility as a speaker while her story entertains and sustains mystery and engagement. Magnetic speakers need to balance information and story. Too much information equates factual-overload and boredom. Too much story, though compelling, affects the speaker's authority on a topic. Like a recipe requires a dash of salt to enhance the flavor, too little leaves behind a bland taste and too much salt overwhelms the palate. Just ask my son when he dumped two tablespoons of salt in a lemon poppyseed muffin batter. I forgave him because he's three, but your audience may not be so forgiving.

CREATIVE PLAY BUILDS MAGNETISM

The backbone for story creation and curiosity is play. The morning of my son's twelfth birthday, his stature is slumped and his countenance morose. I ask, "Why so sad? It's your birthday, a time for celebration. What's wrong?"

With unwavering faith and assurance, he responds, "Mom, my childhood is fleeing before me faster than ever. Now, I'm going to have to work harder to play."

"Work harder to play" uncovers a rich truth. The reality of aging depresses my preteen. I reply, "Adults play."

He says, "But Mom, not often enough."

As a professional consultant, speaker, mother, and spouse, my "should-do" list far outweighs my play list. Play fosters creativity and rests our tired brains of the weighted details. A creative, playful sprit develops magnetic messaging. Even psychologist Jean Piaget researched the importance of play for children's cognitive development, but play shouldn't stop at childhood.

Play engages us into an enjoyable activity and initiates our creative imagination. I define "creativity" as a form of individualized expression, the producing and doing some really cool things fear and pressure-free to make our heart sing. Author and creativity teacher Julia Cameron explains creativity involves radical thinking and is part of our true nature, as creators (2016, 2). The creative process involves a healthy dose of fear and taking risks (Gilbert 2015, 8). As necessary companions to the human condition, creativity and play inspire and evoke magic.

Benefits of Play

Play and exploration grow brain cells. Researchers have evidence concerning brain-derived neurotrophic factor, or "BDNF," a molecule manufactured in our brain essential for the growth and maintenance of brain cells (Dewar 2023). The researcher notes when animals engage in play from investigating with toys, rough-and-tumble play, and other various forms of exploration, BDNF levels increase (Dewar 2023). Playful discovery causes our brain cells to grow and expand.

Studies reveal a link between pretend play and the development of language skills. Researchers analyze thirty-five published studies of the cognitive benefits of play (Quinn, Donnelly, and Kidd 2018). They determine "symbolic play"— what happens when kids use objects to represent other objects—improves cognitive-linguistic and social affective performances. Organized and consistent play works both the brain cognition and emotional connection with others and impacts creative content and delivery style.

STRATEGIES TO FOSTER CREATIVE PLAY

Many adults don't see value in making time to add play to their daily lives. We focus on work and "have-to's." We fear any devotion to play is a waste of time or isn't productive.

We frame play as a thing children, not adults, engage in and worry about making mistakes. Publisher and creativity doula who births creativity out of others, Hollis Citron, says in our podcast conversation, "It's being open to getting dirty, for that gives us permission to make mistakes" (Citron 2022). Intentional play fosters creativity, and creativity stretches limitations to generate new ideas and solve problems. Encountering new experiences through books, travel, and conversations cultivate inventive imagination. Leadership author John Maxwell expands on this notion and explains the importance of eliminating negative thoughts, asking the right questions, developing a creative environment, and spending time with creative people (Maxwell 2017).

Tina's Tips to Engage in Creative Play

Creative play requires openness and intentionality with the body, mind, and spirit.

Engage in physical play: Physical play gets the body to focus on a rhythm, consistent cadence, and washes away the crazy brain chatter and clutter. What kind of physical activities bring you joy? How does your body feel when you move? Do you experience your muscles relax and a slower heart rate when moving? When I dance, cycle, rollerblade, or walk in nature, I feel a calm yet invigorating sensation with each motion. I delight in the nostalgia of jumping on hay bales with the scratchy squish of hay between my toes as laughter flies out of my mouth or the restful petting of goats to invigorate my spirit.

Take time for mental play: Mentally, our brain benefits from play. What happens when you throw a ball or build with Legos?

Does the stress of the world disappear? How do you feel when creating art? Does your heart excitedly bounce with each stroke of paint or crayon? To stretch my mental mind, I read children's books, listen to *The Moth* storytelling podcast, view inspiring art, movies, live concerts, Broadway performances and TED talks, and communicate with other creatives.

Pause inward for spiritual play: Play enables the ability to tune inward and interact with the self. How do you feel doing an obligation-free activity? Do you experience a release of tension, letting go of shallow breath when outdoors and spiritually connecting? Sitting on my sandbar, watching a sunset from my porch or rooftop, meditating, expressing gratitude in my journal, and taking individual trips fuel my soul, clear the monkey mind, and soften worry while increasing the flow of creative juices.

What renews your creative spirit? How do you inspire play and prioritize your imagination? Where is your heart at home and fuels your being? *Sit in your truth and play.*

Curiosity--------Play---------Create!

ADD CREATIVITY TO YOUR PRESENTATION
Magnetic Speakers Go Beyond PowerPoint.

Middle Eastern American keynote speaker Dima Ghawi holds up a glass vase to demonstrate its initial power over her during a 2022 Women Lead Change keynote address. Years prior, her grandmother clutches a flawless, pure vase, stressing Ghawi be perfect. The vase becomes a visual metaphor representing her journey of letting go of perfection.

Her talk doesn't start this way. Ghawi says, "I created a dry speech, very corporate. My friend knew someone who worked with Bill Gates and helped him write a TEDx. They introduced us. After working with a speaking coach for a week, his advice: 'Get rid of the slides.'"

She continues, "My coach helped me build a relationship with the vase, showing the emotional impact of what it represented to me in my life. When I walked away from the vase, it equaled freedom. Near the vase, I felt trapped. I'd build the drama of the speech with story, so the audience can experience the journey with me." At the end of her presentation, Ghawi invites audience members on stage to shatter perfectionism. The audience *becomes part of her talk.*

Additionally, Ghawi gives props away to make her message more memorable. She's passed out jewelry for financial planners to highlight the talk's topic: "We are worth more than gold." She also has thrown coins to a bank audience. The doing and being creative are crucial when developing and presenting content. What inspires your audience? Persuades a new donor for your project? Gains buy-in from your community on a new idea? Motivates your team to listen to the annual report *again*?

Playful presenting can vary from wearing a Mary Poppins costume to persuade community members to donate to the local library to showing visual images of the possibility of a new school addition, to requesting a team member roleplay a scene during an annual report presentation. Consider adding visual aids to make your presentation more creative, playful, and memorable.

Magnetic Speakers Play Using Humor.

Humor Engineer Andrew Tarvin talks about his past internship. His manager requires Tarvin to give a final presentation. His first draft is the standard death by PowerPoint. The night before, he realizes his presentation lacks his creative personality. Tarvin changes his slides last minute, using Microsoft Paint to tell his internship story, complete with surprisingly realistic stick figure visuals of his supervisor and team members. His last slide includes an accurate drawing of the review board, highlighting what's possible if they hire him full-time. He's offered the job, for they love his humor and creativity. Years later, people still mention his memorable talk.

Tarvin provides these insights:

Make the talk more fun for you.

Showcase your individual personality and humorous style.

Take a risk, which can separate you from others.

A client and politician, Cole, explains humor needs to be authentic to the self and speaking situation. In political speeches, Cole says, "I'd incorporate humor in some speeches, yet the humor felt forced, and the audience would notice it felt forced. Humor is an effective tool if done appropriately." Humor must be in alignment with the topic and your authentic speaker style. Trying to be and speak as someone you're not hurts the impact.

Similar to *Goldilocks and the Three Bears,* communicate like Baby Bear—possess the right balance of humor. Speakers can imbed humor in stories, visual aids, and delivery style. Embrace your fun, individual humor.

Magnetic speakers interact with the audience creatively, playfully, and naturally. Be ridiculously curious: magnetic speakers discover their curiosity, build on creativity, and engage in play. If we can identify what "creative" is and feels like, then follow our pulse to create and connect, magnetism happens.

Magnetic speakers do "different."

Curiosity and Creative Play + Ideas + Speaking Your Passion = Change the World.

EXERCISE 1

Flashback to your childhood. What did you enjoy doing? Set the timer for ten minutes and make a list of all the things you found fun. With a highlighter, underline the current appealing activities. From your list, schedule time to play and be creative. Make time for a daily dose of thirty minutes of fun.

Now add a twist: Set an intention prior to the activity. Focus on one project you're in the process of completing. Think of the project prior to your scheduled play. Putting the project in your mind prior, places it in your subconscious. Now, engage in free-spirited play. Following play, return to your project. What bubbles up? Free write/brainstorm project ideas without judgment and see what develops.

EXERCISE 2

Brainstorm a list of ways you can deliver information creatively at monthly or weekly meetings. What stories can you share? Props? Humor? Set aside time to reflect. Remove yourself from distraction. Regularly review your journal.

REFLECTION QUESTIONS

What individual inspired me to be creative as a child? As an adult?

What am I curious about?

What's fun for me?

How did my playdate go? What did I do? How did it feel?

What did I learn today?

What can I do to move forward with a communication or project?

FINDING THE FLOW IN PREPARATION AND PRESENTATION LEADS TO MAGNETIC SPEAKING

Flow is being completely involved in an activity for its own sake. The ego falls away. Time flies. Every action, movement, and thought follows inevitably from the previous one, like playing jazz.

—MIHALY CSIKSZENTMIHALYI, COFOUNDER

OF POSITIVE PSYCHOLOGY

Glancing down at my Fitbit, I'm flabbergasted to see two hours have passed. Buried in the rich study of "speaker presence" for this book, I completely lose track of time. My brain and body are fully focused on only one activity, attentive to the creative act of researching and writing. What I feel these two, fast hours: enjoyment. What I experience? *Flow.*

What is your personal definition of "flow?" Is it going with the flow? Having a certain workflow? Positive psychologist Mihaly Csikszentmihalyi has defined the state of flow to include the following characteristics:

> Balancing challenge and skill
> Feeling control of the skill
> Setting clear goals
> Having a reasonable level of challenge
> Investing intense concentration on meeting goals and adjusting them as conditions change or the challenge elevates
> Receiving feedback from the activity
> Experiencing a distortion of time
> Feeling free of self-consciousness and fear of failure Enjoying the activity for its own sake
>
> (CSIKSZENTMIHALYI 1990, 48-76).

To explore and understand flow and its impact on communication, I interview Dr. Gary Gute and Dr. Deanne Gute who are university flow and positive psychology educators and have collaborated with Mihaly Csikszentmihalyi on flow and creativity research for many years. Dr. Deanne Gute defines flow this way, "Flow happens when someone is completely absorbed in an activity, physically and mentally. Their skills are stretched, and they balance these skills with ability—performing, feeling their best."

She explains flow can come afterward as in the runner's high experience.

Flow is a unique neurological experience when our brains are working most efficiently and seamlessly. Dr. D. Gute says, "Flow creates a nice stew of brain chemicals that makes us feel great. Mihaly always said, 'One taste of flow, you'll want to taste it again.' Flow feels so good because we don't experience it by swallowing a pill or drinking a magic potion. We make it happen with our own attention and effort, our curiosity, our ability to discover patterns and make something from them." The Gutes and I discuss why seeing our own peak performance in flow can be motivating. Flow involves a sense of ecstasy and serenity, an energizing inner clarity, timelessness, and intrinsic motivation. In flow, we're also free of the self-conscious chatter in our heads that prevents us from trying too hard or being too meek and/or random in asserting our ideas.

In flow, we prove to ourselves we can achieve total concentration and goal focus. Purposeful, undistracted communication is more effective and engaging than random and distracted communication. Thinking about my past presentations, the thoughtful preparation, lost concept of time, and deep focus in composing ideas and engaging an audience, I realize these riveting experiences are flow.

MAGNETIC SPEAKERS ACHIEVE FLOW, BOTH IN MESSAGE PREPARATION AND PRESENTATION

Csikszentmihalyi shares with the Gutes there's profound enjoyment in communicating and understanding one another. Dr. D. Gute says, "Communicators can experience flow like a dancer or musician. A speaker can be zoned into the moment, telling a good story, not grasping for words, just connecting with the audience." We discuss magnetic speakers understand their topic fully, lure the audience in, making them laugh, and are more engaged.

As an organic process, flow requires cognitive, conscious effort. A study researches coma patients' damaged brain activity and discovers a connection between a small part of the brainstem and two cortical regions (Fischer et al. 2016). This finding concludes human beings need both arousal and awareness to experience total consciousness and opportunities for flow.

Dr. G. Gute adds, "Mihaly has noted any activity can be flow producing. What's critical is you're experiencing an appropriate level of challenge, no boredom or anxiety. Aptitude of skill and focus are balanced once you identify what the goal is and how you're going to make sure that experience challenges you." For example, we recognize networking is more than just meeting several people. It's possible to make the experience a game: Is it the number of people you're going to meet or number of in-depth conversations you'll have? Attach a clear, challenging goal to the communication.

Authentic public speaking coach Sandra Zimmer researches how public speakers engage in flow (Zimmer n.d.). Zimmer breaks down the four stages of the flow experience: 1) Struggle Stage, 2) Release Stage, 3) Flow Stage, and 4) Recovery Stage. During the struggle stage, the speaker's brain and body produce cortisol and nervous feelings are present. Once speakers detach from the situation, they build to the flow state. Zimmer explains the brain creates positive hormones, which increase the speaker's ability to focus, lowers fear, and elevates mood. During sleep, the final recovery stage provides a calming release.

Dr. D. Gute emphasizes, "Mihaly said, 'The pen is a machine to think with.' As soon as you start writing a speech, you're making order out of chaos, which equals flow. As humans, we need to make order out of chaos. Communication almost always has chaos, for we want to express our ideas and have no idea how. As your attention and topic become more focused, chaos abates." We consider how meaning-making and finding patterns initiates creativity. Flow can be applied in the building and organizing the way we communicate. "[Speakers] experience flow by creating, listening, experiencing, and writing speeches or prepping for a meeting or professional conversation. You either reduce the chaos or feel boredom, which doesn't achieve flow," Dr. D. Gute says. To be magnetic, speakers are aware how they complete tasks, their development process, and means of delivering messages. The communicator must be attentive and have the desire to go deeper, letting go of distractions to fully engage in flow.

Additionally, flow improves skills faster. A study identifies flow participants in the activities of archery, golf, and marksmanship with novice experience improves an average of 28.60 percent compared to 12.22 percent for the control group (Berka et al. 2010). Dr. G. Gute explains, "When we have the experience of flow, the rush of achievement, higher level of skill, and the intrinsic motivation moves us forward one step at a time. This increases our level of achievement and value of flow." This achievement helps the speaker feel a new, good feeling, have purpose, and potentially make a difference.

FLOW IN COMMUNICATION PREPARATION

Flow can lessen anxiety for speakers.

The Gutes mention flow isn't a magical state, nor a switch that flips quickly. Speakers must prepare prior to each communication experience to achieve flow. It helps to begin with an awareness of which communication contexts make you feel empowered and energized versus those you feel self-conscious, even anxious. Speakers need as much intentional practice to overcome anxious situations. Confidence and the possibility flow wins over anxiety increases with practice. Communication situations and conditions either encourage or kill flow.

We address how networking poses challenges, especially for introverts. Understanding flow conditions helps. As a speaker, I narrow the experience into smaller, manageable goals to lessen my self-consciousness and anxiety. Instead of worrying about the whole room, I break it down into quadrants to "find the Dale in the room." "Working the room" is more intimidating than meeting one person at a time. Entering the space, I focus on these questions: Who can I approach? What do I want to learn? Chipping away, I make the challenge reasonable. Magnetism comes from being organized and getting others to share your goals and cultivate positive relationships. As a speaker, you set the tone.

Human beings are resistant to change. Often, leaders find themselves sharing a new vision to their teams, and the newness and abstract idea may be too much for their team to absorb. Using a framework helps. Dr. G. Gute says, "Connect with smaller goals, verbalizing goals along the way to link to the bigger vision. This reduces anxiety. Ask: Do we share that vision? How do we share that vision?" Delivering more presentations and building relationships increase trust and lessens fear.

To achieve flow, it takes productive intention.

Productivity expert and author Cal Newport mentions the importance of humans valuing and engaging in deep work. Newport defines deep work as "professional activities performed in a state of distraction-free concentration that push your cognitive capabilities to their limit. These efforts create new value, improve your skill, and are hard to replicate" (2016, 3). He cites the human challenge of fighting desires all day long, yet deep work allows individuals to quickly master hard things and produce at an elite level both in quality and speed (Newport 2016, 29). To reach our fullest potential requires cultivating a deep work habit.

Deep work involves a certain cadence, intentionality, and a give and take in your schedule. To produce great work takes intense focus and scheduling longer blocks of time. Comedian Jerry Seinfeld crafts jokes through his daily ritual of "not breaking the chain." On a calendar, Seinfeld marks an "x" each day he writes. The "x's" motivate him to make daily progress on tasks and increases his productivity to compose funnier jokes. Magnetic speakers prioritize daily time to be in higher level, abstract, creative thinking, and engage in deep work frequently.

Additionally, author Dan Charnas writes modeling chefs' means of work improves productivity and addresses the French philosophy of mise-en-place, "to put in place" (2016,

27). Chefs establish a clear process, place materials in a specific space, and work clean. Charnas expresses we need to balance two types of tasks: process (responding and writing emails, paying invoices, etc.) and immersive (creative thinking, writing, etc.) (2016, 108). He highlights the importance of planning, determining clear action steps, and creating a sensible, sequential order to achieve a goal. Again, flow and creating a clear, engaging idea and presentation involve immersive process and productive intention.

To achieve flow, create an individualized system.

Prior to presenting a keynote, Dr. D. Gute asks organizers about the audience, other speakers, the goal, setting, and if there's food. Understanding the space and context prepares a speaker's mind to adapt their style and minimize distractions. Dr. G. Gute stresses they have different speaking styles and acknowledges Deanne's meticulous method. Her methodical patterned work demands time, and she adheres to a consistent plan prior, arranging his part.

Dr. G. Gute says, "Flow is the creator of communication. There are phases to any creative progress. There's no one way. Process equals preparation. There's a period of struggle. A piece you've mastered goes through the evaluation stage, then we switch the brain to be critical in edit mode, and finally transition into incubation." We validate the importance of a clear process of research, revision, and hard work to have the authority to speak.

To achieve flow, work fast.

Dr. G. Gute explains, "The idea of working fast has benefits. We can produce better work with intense practice. Instead of getting bogged down in all the planning and thinking, just do it." Developing creative ideas can be painfully slow at times. He quotes writer and coach Alex Mathers, "The best ideas arise out of an inner wisdom that comes through the space between thoughts." The process can be daunting. Magnetic speakers just get started. They write and write fast.

To achieve flow, allow spaciousness, relaxation, and take breaks.

Dr. D. Gute says, "We're so conditioned to be busy and produce. You can't produce something good all the time nor always be in the thinking mode." Dr. G. Gute adds, "Allow the field to fallow. You can't produce crops 365 days a year. It's the same with an idea. You can't do flow all the time. Intense effort has to be balanced with relaxation. Flow is the revising of the communication." Yet, it's okay to take a break. They mention Csikszentmihalyi says creativity is a mysterious time. If uninspired, choose an activity that exerts less effort. I've walked outdoors, taken a shower, or pet a goat. Speakers need space between thoughts.

FLOW CONDITIONS TO PREPARE A PRESENTATION
Create a clear goal: What's your speaking purpose? To inform? Persuade? Motivate or inspire?

Balance challenge and skill: Match your passion for the topic by learning as much as you can. Develop your ability to appeal to different audience learning styles (audible, visual, kinesthetic, written).

Use clear and immediate feedback from the work itself: observe and record cues to tell if you're doing well (internal—feelings within—and external—cues watching and listening to your audience's responses).

Design a system and workspace to facilitate deep concentration and creation. Remember flow and creativity require a mix of working slow and deliberately, with working fast and unconsciously, with not working at all.

Tina's Tips: Flow Principles for Communication Preparation and Developing Clients

1. Time block a work schedule. I schedule two hours each day to engage in deep, immersive work.

2. Select the best, consistent thinking time to encourage flow. Mornings are best for me because I'm fully rested, highly energized, and feel freshest.

3. Set the stage. Select a favorite beverage, music (if you like background noise), close the door, and turn off phone and computer notifications to eliminate distractions. When working with clients or creative projects, I set a timer to be fully present in the moment, in control of my time.

4. Create a clear goal to achieve during the immersive work. Am I creating a presentation outline? Researching the topic? Practicing?

5. Commit to a schedule and stick to it.

ACHIEVING FLOW WHEN PRESENTING

With a last PowerPoint click, my eight-hour management training presentation comes to a close. Amazed at the speed of the day and engagement with the group, I ask operation's managers: "What questions do you have for me?" One manager raises his hand and asks, "How do you present like that all day?" When I request he clarifies the question, I learn this manager is curious about how I present for such a long time, full of energy and connection to the audience. I respond, "I love the topic and make the presentation about my audience, tailoring the message to meet their needs." When speakers set an intention, are audience-centered, and love what they say and do, they experience flow. Even when there are surprises.

Magnetic Speakers Are Adaptable.

Dr. G. Gute speaks of flow as adapting minute by minute to meet the changing demands of a challenging situation. For a past keynote presentation, the Gutes expect a standard meeting room with a conventional seating arrangement. Instead, they present in a space like an airline hangar. This surprising set-up suddenly makes their keynote less formal and requires a different approach.

Halfway through the presentation, the Gutes are in the speaker zone. Suddenly, they hear a jarring sound like a garage door slamming up and down. People wearing hard hats clang and march past. Once this interesting interlude finishes, both speakers continue. The more speakers prepare and practice, the more composed they are in stressful or unpredictable situations. As Dr. G. Gute says, "To achieve flow, be well-prepared—but adapt."

The Gutes' speaking experience reflects all flow components: Time is distorted. Self-consciousness doesn't get the best of them. Every step is intuitive and organic. They have self-control due to preparation, no fumbling through notes or trouble deciding what to do next.

Magnetic Speakers Are Relatable.

A core principle of flow is the less we're focused on ourselves, the more we engage successfully in a challenge and the more we enjoy it. Dr. D. Gute examines ways they create genuine relationships and relatability with their audience. Because of the unexpected informality and close audience contact, they decide to become acquainted with the group. Dr. G. Gute asks them: "What is something that fascinates you?" This questions links to their keynote topic, which is creating conditions for college students to experience flow in the classroom. Both speakers purposefully engage the audience and prep them to listen by first attending to their responses and later referring to their examples in the talk. This helps build flow and audience connection.

Magnetic Speakers Respond to Feedback.

How do you know if you're engaging the audience? How do you keep building those skills?

Dr. D. Gute explains the importance of watching facial expressions and nonverbal cues and requesting audience feedback in a survey form. If the audience has been in flow with the speaker, their curiosity ignites. Speakers see curiosity reflected in their questions. Perhaps they've experienced moments not in flow but in confusion. Their questions will tell you that too. Reading nonverbal cues and listening to verbal feedback help a speaker adjust in real time and create a memorable audience experience.

We address setting limits to our attention. It's possible for a speaker to be in total flow with a topic, leaving the audience behind. Whether presentations, meetings, team projects or conversations, we must pick up and act on the feedback from whomever we're trying to connect with. When speakers are in the planning and creating stage, the goals need to reflect the interests and needs of the audience. If they do, flow is more likely mutual.

Magnetic speakers create powerful connections and lasting impacts.

Dr. G. Gute mentions, "Years ago, Mihaly spoke of attending a talk, and the presenter mentioned flying saucers. Carl Young, the psychologist, triggers Mihaly's fascination with psychology and pushes him to ask more questions, eventually developing what we now know as 'flow.' That one speech really changed his life and his life's work."

To summarize, flow does the following:

Engages the mind and body

Helps us make complex connections

Keeps us focused on the audience instead of ourselves and what people are thinking about us

Keeps the audience engaged

Cures boredom for the audience and anxiety for the speaker

Involves cycles and stages: Planning, preparation, gathering resources, ideation, intense effort, relaxation, incubation, evaluation.

HABITS FOR CULTIVATING FLOW: DR. DEANNE AND DR. GARY GUTE'S RECOMMENDATIONS FOR SPEAKERS

1. Journal or keep an idea log. For two minutes every day, jot down questions, topic ideas, or thoughts on helping people understand a problem. Focus on the mindset, "I can build on this later." When you visit your journal, you'll never feel blocked or out of ideas.

2. Sketch out a mental model of what you're going to do to divide and conquer to complete tasks in advance of your event. Visualize yourself doing the items on your to-do list by telling yourself, "I'll remember to…"

3. Visualize the environment you'll be speaking, and present what you're going to say in your head, playing it out like a movie in your mind. Create a set of safety nets to deal with the "what if's" and worry. Visualizing speaking your entire presentation imprints your content in your consciousness to boost memory, reduce chaos, and free up your energy during the presentation to focus on the emotion behind your words to play off audience reactions.

4. Take time the day before to fully prepare yourself for a successful experience. Start by reiterating the goals

you're planning to achieve. Sleep. Incubate. This sets you up for success.

5. Rehearse out loud. Good rehearsals make flow more likely to happen at the event.

6. Focus on the experience, not the outcome. Going in with a curious, playful mindset can help free from worry of others' judgments and open up new modes of thinking and problem-solving.

7. If you're in a meeting or other two-way or group conversation, use more open-ended questions than statements. Focus on being *interested*, not *interesting*. Relationship-building with your topic or idea and your audience begins with genuine curiosity questions and openness to learning. The more involved we get and the more attention we invest, the more likely we are to experience flow rather than frustration.

KEY TAKEAWAYS FOR FLOW IN COMMUNICATION

As speakers, we can experience the flow state in both our preparation and presentation of our message. We want our audiences to share the optimal experience. If we plan, create, and stage with the interests and needs of the audience in mind, and we genuinely engage with them when we speak, the audience will engage with us. That's what it means to be magnetic. Getting there requires clear intention. It demands diligence. It requires knowing the content inside and out to speak with confidence and fluency. It requires practice. This chapter discusses ways you set the stage prior, during, and after your communication.

Explore spaces to unleash your inner creator. Do you prefer quiet or noise? Indoors or outdoors? Typing on the computer or handwriting with a pen? A combination? Once you identify the space and strategies for crafting your message, write fast. Write slow. Eventually your heart will send the right signals to your brain and inner passion and purpose will start showing up on the page. Flush out your thoughts. Work hard. Take breaks and step back. Revise many times. Practice and practice frequently.

Balance the rules and systems with adaptability. When the time comes to speak your ideas to your given audience, meet them where they are. Walk into the space anchored in your confidence. Your preparation is part of you. Listen to your intuition and breathe your ideas out. Like an athlete enters the game ready to play with heart, as the speaker, you're like a dancer in flow, conversation will feel natural and effortless. You've created a specific, challenging goal. You're looking for feedback. Use it. In any conversation or presentation, we set limits on our attention. We need to be aware of the audience's limited attention. It's possible for a speaker to be in total flow with a topic, leaving the audience behind. Whether it's a presentation, meeting, team project, or networking event, picking up and acting on the feedback you're getting will help you achieve more flow. Flow leads to creative thought and connected, magnetic speaking.

Remember, your flow doesn't just happen; you create it with your own effort.

EXERCISES

1. Take risks and shift your perspective by doing new (creativity class, cooking, driving, or hiking a new space, etc.).

2. Set a goal for an upcoming meeting or speaking event. Create a plan, leverage your knowledge, skills, and experiences, then self-monitor.

3. Think of a prior presentation you felt flow. What was that moment like for you? What was the overall speaking context? How did you feel about the topic? Journal about the experience. Picture a future speaking engagement. Write three goals for how you'll accomplish flow in preparation and the presentation. Contact a friend or colleague to hold you accountable and debrief with them following the presentation. Did you meet the goals you set for yourself?

REFLECTION QUESTIONS

Have I experienced flow?

How did it feel? What was it like? What was I doing? My process?

Have I witnessed a speaker in flow? What was it like as an audience member?

What's my goal for the next speaking experience to achieve flow?

PART III

YOUR MAGNETIC MECHANICS

AM I PREPARED TO BE THE INSTRUMENT OF MY OWN MESSAGE?

I believe in playing around with things (and people) rather than trying to control them. I am fascinated by the absurdity of our attempts to control everything around us—particularly other people. I want us to be able to learn to enjoy uncertainty, rather than dread it. After all, the unknown is the source of many of our greatest delights— surprise, creativity, identity, a sense of agency and so on.

—ROBERT POYNTON

On my first day of Level I Improvisation, the instructor informs us we're performing our final class on stage in front of friends, family, and strangers. Even with a theatre background, this new knowledge looms in my head with dread. How will I trust these new people in such a short time? Throughout the eight-week seminar, we learn the foundational rule of improv: "Yes-and."

My instructor tells us "yes-and" means accepting the other and the moment as it occurs, then add something to the scene.

During the improvisation performance, all of us stand stiffly in a single line at the back of the stage waiting. Bright spotlights illuminate a brave team member who requests a suggestion from the audience. An even more courageous performer leaps from the backline and starts to wave her hands back and forth horizontally.

Time passes. No one steps forward to support her. After an excruciatingly, long pause, my two feet move ahead suddenly and join her. Together we create a scene in a massage parlor.

Following the show, animated and proud, I exclaim, "How fun! I enjoyed developing a scene with you."

She grins and responds, "Yes, even though initially, I was preparing pizza dough."

My partner lets go of the attachment to the scene she creates in her mind. She makes me look good. She trusts the present moment, her partner, and who she is to produce something new and different. *She lets go and personifies "yes-and."*

BEING FULLY PRESENT IS MAGNETIC

Professor and improvisation facilitator Robert Poynton has created a "yes-and" triangle composed of three elements: Let go; notice more; use everything (Taylor and Stewart 2022). These three "yes-and" principles apply to communicating with others in a more magnetic way.

LET GO

Magnetism requires letting go of past thoughts, future ideas, fears, judgment of self and others, and the negative stories we tell ourselves. Our internal stories influence how others see and hear the message. To let go, identify, and label the thought. Breathe out the fear and breathe in spacious clarity. Visualize a happy place: a sunny, sandy beach, cozy, soft couch, or tall, shady tree. Stand firm in the present moment. Describe your comfortable space. Do you feel less overwhelmed or cramped with worry? Are you noticing tension softening in your shoulders, arms, and legs? Is your head clear? If you let go of the mind's chatter and be present, you connect more completely. The audience will feel it.

NOTICE MORE

Be fully present. Listen and attend to the moment as it occurs. Who is present with you? Is it a supervisor? Team member? New client? What time of day is it? What's the context? Enter the communication without an agenda, open to change. Tune into your body and explore how interesting the person and moment are. Be intentional and tend to their needs: Do they want informed instruction? Inspiration or motivation? A listening ear?

USE EVERYTHING

Accept the moment and other person as is. Are you experiencing stuck feelings or expectations of how the conversation or presentation should go? Avoid this through investigating what's possible and releasing the need to jump to conclusions and be right or get others to agree. Observe their voice and body language. What do their facial expressions and tone of voice tell you about their values?

Knowledge, experiences, and background influence communication and connection. Every communication involves a social and content layer (Quintanilla and Wahl 2014, 41). As social creatures, we're influenced by our experiences with people. A past conflict can affect and shape the next interaction.

What's your point of concentration? How will you use your body? Present your idea to connect with your audience?

Let go of control. Get good with uncertainty. Trust yourself.

In a networking conversation with FLY artist Ted Barr, he reviews his style of art: "Don't fall in love with the first layer." FLY art lets go of control. We discuss embracing the unexpected. He explains we're taught as children to stay in the lines, which develops a perfectionistic attitude and hurts creativity. Barr expresses the need to emerge beyond the lines and explore innovative ideas.

Speaking is an art, a flow of energy. Barr highlights it's becoming and transforming as we're creators. Enjoy the journey. His number one FLY rule: stay out of the lines and say "yes" to dare and create art out of your comfort zone. He emphasizes, "Being at the center of your true essence is free, radical self-expression." Communicating with confidence and clarity is being in your essence. It's feeling and being free. Barr ends, "Apply brightness and light in what we write and speak." Using your imagination, play with your message and add personal flare, a visual aid, story, or audience participation. When I introduce my business, I hold up a large magnet to emphasize the dynamic results clients get from completing my Magnetic Speaker Blueprint Coaching Program.

Let go. Let in the present moment. Be.

IMPROVISATION TRAINING IMPROVES COMMUNICATION

Humor Engineer Andrew Tarvin shares his best friend gently pushes him into performing improvisation. Tarvin discusses improv games provide structure, and structure assists with creativity and the "yes-and" mindset. While he's skeptical at first, from audience feedback, he realizes he must be at least a little funny as a stand-up comedian given he actually makes audiences laugh. It's only through practice and repetition he becomes less nervous. Tarvin evolves from not eating all day before a show because of his nerves to ten shows later, waiting half a day without eating, to building the skill and projecting confidence to where he can eat on stage if he needs to. Tarvin says, "Practice and repetition of the improvisation skill three times a week is gifting yourself the inner discipline to have a safe space, something I couldn't rely on myself."

Author and improvisation trainer, Bob Kulhan, explains improvisation practice and training is a results-driven approach to communication (2017, 44). Improvisation trains participants to postpone judgment, suspend critiquing and overanalyzing, and remain positive; all increase possibilities for success. He states, "If you make a conscious effort to change the way you think about something, your speech will reflect it." Kulhan clarifies we allow certain barriers to hold us back from effective communication: the fear of losing control of the situation and uncertainty, status of audience members, or insufficient motivation (2017). The improvisation skill conquers the fear by slowing the brain's insecure inner chatter and self-deprecating thoughts to be the confident self, fully in the moment.

Psychotherapist, writer/performer Jude Treder-Wolff says, "Improv training is one of the most effective ways to access this heart full of 'yes.' To create in real time with no plan, no props, no script, and no director requires a commitment to the moment unique to the improv experience. We can learn to say 'yes' out loud by the way we play with other people, accepting their ideas and trying them out. Our creative courage grows when we risk engaging with people in this way, and that fuels a useful resilience to real-life stresses and pressures. It's an interesting paradox we unlock, the genius within ourselves by treating others as if they are brilliant."

"The Five Improv Elements to Personal Growth and Creative Expansion:

Direct experience
Emotional engagement
Focus
Uncertainty within structure heightens attention
Effort and engagement links to reward"

(TREDER-WOLFF 2023).

Improvisation classes help me overcome internal censors and inhibitions. Playing a character, creating a scene, and speaking dialogue on the spot works my brain in a whole new way. From acting as Jack and the Bean Stock's brother to Cinderella's stepsister, or a bird increases my creative, playful courage. Personal growth involves commitment to the choice to place yourself in uncertain experiences to stretch attention and train you to focus and listen. Playing a variety of characters on stage with others closes the gap of reaction time. Because I choose to practice and put in the effort, my creativity and imaginative problem-solving skills expand, my ability to surrender grows, and I accept the moment as is.

Improving presence through improvisation training requires action on your part. Find a theatre, comedy club, or educational institution. Sign up for an improv class. Step on the stage. Once you receive a one-word suggestion, commit to a character and listen to your partner and agree to what truths they've created on stage. Here's where the fun comes: add something to move the scene forward. Respond through action and/or dialogue without over-thinking. The more real you are, the more interesting the scene becomes. Let go of the notion of mistakes. Instead, see them as opportunities, and play.

Letting go is a choice, a practice, a discipline, and a mindset. Magnetic speakers let go of the past, focus on the present, and trust themselves.

BENEFITS OF IMPROVISATION TRAINING
Improvisation lessens fear.

"You're not going to make it if you don't speak up. You're smart, but you don't raise your hand or speak," declares a Catholic priest to AgArts Executive Director and author Mary Swander when she's in second grade. Swander continues her story, explaining her teacher assigns her to present a demonstration speech. Swander selects the value of dairy-added products. "Kids went to sleep, for I spoke in such a soft voice. My teacher said, 'This kid's not going to make it.'"

As a child, Swander hears adults say she's smart but needs to speak up and more often. She doesn't talk to teachers, children, or people in general and is born with selective mutism, a "complex childhood anxiety disorder characterized by a child's inability to speak and communicate effectively in select social settings" (Shipon-Blum n.d.). Yet, her Irish Catholic family sings and tells stories and jokes. Terrified of any social interaction, she remembers running to her grandmother's side of the house to hide while her mother hosts coffees.

Eventually, her parents enroll Swander in acting classes at a children's theatre. For weeks, she doesn't open her mouth. The director assigns her the role of the wicked queen. "It was horrible. I fell off the stage, but I got through it. It took years. Theatre taught me to be a different human. Find the fun in it. When I got older, I'd think on my feet and even teach classes. It took centering myself, breathing, for I'm nervous every day. I have to tell myself, just enjoy this. Connect with people. Tell myself to be a different person." This attitude, the façade of playing a character on stage, translates well for Swander to communicate with real people in real-life offstage.

Swander still struggles with nervousness and finds speaking scary, yet she lets go of the resistance. She pretends she's sitting on her couch comfortably teaching or conversing casually with friends. Swander emphasizes the specific training in theatre and her continued practice comfort her strong fear to communicate to various audiences.

Improvisation training improves your brain function.

Clay Drinko, PhD, explains the increased coherence of brain function through the practice of "yes-and'ing" (2021). Drinko cites the 2008 Limb study, which finds improvisation improves jazz musician's creativity and expands their memory.

In a neuroscience study, researchers Mary DeMichele and Scott Kuenneke conduct pre- and post-assessments to analyze teen's brain function and nervous system, specifically those who experienced trauma (2021). They observe an increase in coherence from the pre-assessment to the post-assessment from individuals who experience improvisation training. Teens who engage in "yes-and" training display more integrated and effective responses. They attribute the brain's effective function and integration of timely communication to improv's "yes-and" rule, which creates a sense of safety by limiting uncertainty during social interactions (DeMichele and Kuenneke 2021).

Improvisation enhances creativity and problem-solving skills.

Practicing improvisation helps with idea-creation. Researchers assess stressed participants who engage in a two-hour, six-week improv workshop (Schwenke et al. 2020). They evaluate the questionnaires and surveys prior and following the study, measure the participant's resilience, self-efficacy, self-esteem, acceptance, mindfulness, and creativity. After six weeks of improv lessons, the study concludes participants increase creativity and measure more divergent thinking to solve problems, breaking ingrained patterns of behavior. Creative and resourceful solutions strengthen a speaker's content and overall connection with others when communicating.

In college classes, I've facilitated the improvisation game One Word Story. After requesting a suggestion from the class, students create a story together, one word at a time. When we debrief, students are amazed at how hard they're trying to be the funniest or most clever, thinking versus being, and not letting go of the goo in their heads. They discover richer stories are developed through presence, openness, absent control, and perfectionism. By "yes-and'ing" each other, together, they co-create the second story clearly and confidently.

Improvisation increases trust and acceptance.

Finally, improvisation leads to more trust, acceptance, and a deeper presence (Gesell 2015). During a 2015 Applied Improvisation Network Conference workshop, facilitator and improviser Izzy Gesell discusses the importance of practicing improvisation. Gesell emphasizes the "yes-and" skill teaches the ability to locate a point of concentration, to surrender and allow the moment to reveal itself. Magnetism necessitates trusting the self and the moment as it occurs. Drinko ends his article, stating "[...] improv allows people to shift from whatever state they're in to a more optimal state where they feel coherent and connected" (2021). This practice assists speakers to think deeply and connect at an intimate level.

"YES-AND" ENERGY AND ATTITUDE

Pulling the large, white envelope from my mailbox, I enthusiastically rip it open to discover I've been accepted as a Walt Disney World cast member for the twenty-fifth anniversary as an attractions host in the Magic Kingdom. My only exposure to Disney includes TV commercials with Cinderella's majestic castle as the backdrop. Disney's imagineers transform the castle into a Pepto Bismal-pink Candy Land structure, complete with multiple gum drops, lollipops, and candy canes.

Weeks later, supervisor Hector, a kind man whose smile fills his face, announces to our team backstage, "How do you feel about the Disney Castle?" Silence and blank stares fill the room. Following the lengthy pause, he asks again.

One seasoned cast member expresses a dislike for the terrible marketing decision. Others point out the challenge of reassuring guests this design isn't permanent. After listening to disgruntled opinions and concerns, Hector says, "Thank you for sharing your opinions. Now, what can we do? Let's think about our guests. Let's make it about them. We are here because of them. Let's listen to their concerns. Acknowledge how they feel and give them hope. Emphasize we care about their opinion, and we're so happy they're here to celebrate with us. Let's work on *our energy and attitude*."

Hector's *"yes-and" attitude* converts our communication to focus on the needs of guests and how Disney cast members communicate with one another about the castle. "Yes-and" embodies a positive, open mindset, accepts the other and the moment as it happens, and adds to it. Like Hector, decide and commit to communicate fully present as an active, unbiased listener, and meet your audience where they are.

Magnetism requires being fully present. Let go. Notice more. Use everything.

EXERCISES

Take an improv class. Explore local comedy clubs, universities, or theatres for guided training. While there are online options, I recommend in-person classes. Second City and UBC Training Center provide great options nationwide.

Play improv games with friends and colleagues for personal and professional development. Improv provides multiple benefits: detaching from expectations, overcoming self-judgment and fear of failure, improving listening skills, and encouraging spontaneity and imagination to generate new ideas.

Game suggestions: One Line Story, Taboo, Mad Libs, Outburst, Truth or Dare. When you participate in improv games, an individual's sense of humor shines. You may feel pure enjoyment and amusement from developing newly created stories and scenes with little to no preparation. Guessing the words on the list within a time limit in Taboo or Outburst or choosing words for Mad Libs encourages less judgment, gut responses, and explores possibilities. Improvisation initiates imaginative stories, conversation, and not to mention lots of laughter, in a fun, playful way. It's the perfect blend of joy with the edge of fear to expand your communication skills.

Websites offering improv game suggestions:

Team Building

Session Lab (Smart 2021)

REFLECTION QUESTIONS

Explore your metacognition: think about your thinking. What am I saying to myself? How does my mental tape function? What would it feel like to let go?

How can I "yes-and" at work? With different relationships? Projects?

Recall a moment when you felt a project wasn't perfect enough or enough in general. How did I feel? How did others respond? How will I react differently next time? How can I let go of my attachment to perfection?

Do I have an unfinished presentation or idea I want to present to my boss or team holding me back from making real change?

What issues, problems, or concerns do I have about speaking/communicating with others?

How will I let go? Notice more? Use everything?

THE WHO THAT WE MOVE: POISE IS A VERB

How you are put together must be a
metaphor for your message.

—ERIN DUFFY, PRESENCE COACH

At twelve years old, I invest long hours of piano practice to perform with meticulous perfection at a competition, three classical pieces, major and minor scales, all free of knuckle-gripping anxiety. Weeks later, at church, I place my hands on the keys and hammer out the first four stanzas of Handel's Minuet in D Major. Forgetting the Minuet, I play the same four stanzas repeatedly and stand by the piano and bow. I exemplify my piano teacher's adage: Be poised. Start and end strong and do your best.

During the pandemic, I present my first in-person workshop in over a year. My shoulders tense and my heartbeat races a mile a minute. Hands shaking, I strap a mask over my nose and mouth. My piano teacher Thelma's voice rings in my ears, "Don't 'B' flat. Don't 'B' sharp. Just 'B' natural." I think: "Start and end strong. Do your best." After a deep breath, the nervous butterflies in my stomach spin into a calmer formation. I march into the speaking space with a newfound self-assurance. This experience stresses: trust your voice and body to support the message.

That's poise.

The Oxford Dictionary defines poise as "a calm and confident manner with control of your feelings or behavior" (2023). Poise balances movement and vocal choices. Improvement shifts the thinking and engages in specific action. By first steadying the mind, the speaker stabilizes their voice with their body to achieve desired results. Poise establishes your credibility and image.

I'll explain basic elements of poise and provide examples and exercises to illustrate confidence.

It starts with the mind.

Then with the voice.

And, finally, aligning your message with the body.

EXAMPLES OF POISED SPEAKERS
Poet Maya Angelou opens President Clinton's 1993 inauguration with a compelling poem, reaching the large crowd with her deep, rich voice. She expresses her powerful poetic style with intense

vocal projection, passionate upright posture, and emotional facial expressions to showcase her sense of belonging, expressing fully the Maya she is. Contrast her style with Tina Fey's witty sense of humor, powerful pauses, and quirky facial expressions when she accepts the 2010 Mark Twain Award. Finally, speaker Anne Lamott's smooth, fluid, and conversational vocal style complement her comfortable stance as she welcomes the audience into her heart and humor during her TED talk (Lamott 2012). Each of these women use their voice and body in the space, gracefully and elegantly as the self they are.

The above speakers achieve a state of balance, a dignified, self-confident composure, stability, and unwavering determination with their vocal and physical delivery. Magnetic speakers do the work and align their vocal and physical choices with messages to get the results.

Poise is a verb.

ACHIEVE POISED PRESENCE
How do you achieve poised presence when presenting on stage? Leading a meeting? Introducing yourself to a new client?

Author James Clear highlights the importance of identifying the process to focus on the outcomes you desire with these two steps:

1. "Decide the type of person you want to be.

2. Prove it to yourself with small wins, then break your bad habit(s)" (Clear n.d.).

Behavioral change impacts your identity. Be aware of your internal tape. Change your inner dialogue from, "I'm nervous about this meeting/presentation" or "I don't want to do this" to "I'm excited to meet new people" or "I'm ready to share and hear new ideas." The difference between fear and excitement is the energy and attention we place on the thought.

Visiting researcher Lakshmi Balachandra analyzes successful business pitches and notes the strongest indicator for entrepreneurs to earn investors doesn't include the speaker's credentials or speech content but their traits of confidence, comfort level, and passionate enthusiasm (Cuddy 2015, 19). Social psychologist Amy Cuddy emphasizes this as speaker's *presence*, which she defines as "the state of being attuned to and able to comfortably express our true thoughts, feelings, values, and potential" (2015, 24).

Additionally, a qualitative study describes nurses lack confidence when communicating with physicians. Researchers conclude listening to negative stories of physician's behaviors and having a gap in preparation influence nurses' confidence (Forbes and Evans 2022). Hearing other nurses' horror stories negatively affects future levels of self-assuredness when communicating. This study emphasizes our level of poise is influenced by what we hear, the stories we tell ourselves, and how much or little we prepare.

How do we focus on positive, internal dialogue?

Explore what intuitive author and speaker Abraham Hicks calls "segment intending." Segment intending involves awareness of you in your surroundings, what's happening, and defining the moment's intentions (Mariolle 2021). Pause prior to each speaking experience. Allow transition time from one context to the next. Setting a clear intention at least ten minutes prior to any speaking engagement provides ample mental preparation. This transition time allows the speaker to step into a confident, clear mindset, ready to speak. Decide prior how to be in the moment.

Answer the following questions:

Who is my audience?

What is my objective with this audience?

What do they need?

Believe, write, and say this affirmation: *I will give this audience my full attention and actively listen.* Transform the negative noise and emotional dread to positive energy. When speakers act on positive thought, they create new vocal and physical behaviors to sound, feel, and be more attractive to their audience.

THE POISED, MAGNETIC VOICE

Your voice is a powerful, influential instrument. While the mask changes my appearance, it doesn't affect my impact. I articulate the words and project my voice. With fluid gestures, my body leans into the words, exhibits positive energy, and complements the voice. For two hours, this presentation becomes a lovely dance sequence between the audience's thoughtful discussion questions and the speaker's supportive responses.

Let go of the myths of how you've defined your voice. These myths range from believing you're born with a bad voice to your vocal quality can't be fixed. Instead heighten your awareness and lean into the belief: *This topic and audience matter to me.*

Identify the type of speaker you are. Voice coach Barbara McAfee explains five distinct vocal sounds in her TEDx Talk: Earth, fire, water, metal, and air.

Earth: low, slow, deeper quality
Fire: loud, dramatic, projecting passion
Water: warm, flowing, comforting
Metal: bright, sharp, cutting through, amplified
Air: light, inspiring, airy

(MCAFEE 2016).

McAfee highlights we have a primary vocal style we're born with; however, we can pepper in other styles (2016). Magnetic speakers are deliberate with their vocal choices. Our voice reveals more than our mood; it shapes others' perceptions of our health, education, confidence level, and overall state of being. For example, if you feel your voice isn't being heard, frustrated, you may amplify into a metal vocal style, even if your natural quality is more earthy.

What vocal style am I?

Evaluate your vocal tone and cadence. Is your tone naturally louder dynamics or softer intonation? Are you more expressive or calm and deliberative with your speech? Do you speak at a rapid or slower pace?

Compare Barack Obama's slower pace and lengthy pauses to Tony Robbins's louder, larger overall vocal presence. Where do you fall on the vocal spectrum? What elements of your voice do you use to emphasize a point? While the earth element claims authority, or the fire style pumps on the passion, the airy style draws people in with story and persuades audiences to choose to listen. Magnetism demands identifying and embodying your vocal style and brand.

In Dr. Wendy LeBorgne's TEDx Talk, she associates branding the voice with others' perceptions (LeBorgne 2018). The five vocal elements include intensity, inflection, rate, frequency, and quality. Negative pitch perceptions range from aggressive to boring, condescending, or less intelligent. For example, raising the pitch at the end of a sentence indicates you're asking a question rather than making a declarative statement. Therefore, be aware of where and how you emphasize words.

Be Vocally Authentic.

Andy Mort, podcaster and coach, shares the importance of self-reflection. Listening to past podcasts, Mort notices his vocal tone and delivery change a lot. He states, "There was a harshness, holding tightly, an intensity. I wasn't listening to the interviewees. I was thinking during the interview, 'How can I make this work?' I went from massively preparing to trusting instead, flowing into the conversation. Preparation helped me touch on certain points." Vocally poised speakers balance how much to prepare. They speak as if they're in a conversation and trust themselves and their ability.

Mort expresses the importance of finding the song in the speech with rhythm, vocal dynamics, and pacing. "There's a crescendo where a message reaches a heightened state of energy, and then a moment of silence. A whisper. And that is where the connection occurs." Magnetic speakers raise and lower their energy to co-create their message with the audience. Just like a choir varies their vocal dynamics to add beautiful texture to their song, so must the speaker when they speak.

MAGNETIC SPEAKERS VARY THEIR VOCAL PACE

Martin Luther King Jr. applies a variety of rhetorical devices to educate, engage, and excite his audience. King varies the ebb and flow of his message. He speeds up pace to share deep enthusiasm for his dream and deliberately slows his pace to convince the audience to act.

Magnetic speakers are strategic with their vocal rate. They slow their pace for data, new information, or a calculated, persuasive call to action, and accelerate for easier content to comprehend stories, questions, and examples. Spaciousness imparts power. Consider three lengths of pauses: short, medium, and long length.

Short pause, a one-beat breath=aesthetics for your message, adding texture. Previous host of the *Daily Show*, Trevor Noah provides comedic relief with his short pauses when he changes his vocal tone with different character dialects.

Medium pause, a two-three-beat breath=offer audience think time, cognition to focus on the main point. Brené Brown allows audience response after her opening story in her vulnerability TEDx speech. She pauses for audiences to laugh and understand her self-definition as a researcher and storyteller.

Long pause, longer than a three-beat breath=engage emotional appeal; MLK's "I Have a Dream" speech uses dramatic pauses to ring home his American Dream of equality.

It's the speaker's job to keep the audience in the know. Slow your cadence for data or harder to comprehend material. When the audience understands information, their empowerment increases. Ask yourself, what overall quality does your voice have? If your voice is hoarse frequently, assess your breathing patterns and level of anxiety. Additionally, avoid vocalized pauses such as "ums," "ahs," "ya knows," "you guys," etc. These filler words distract and hurt a speaker's credibility. Assess your verbal fillers with the following questions:

When do I do it?

How often do I do it?

Why do I do it?

I've witnessed audience members tally the amount of vocalized pauses a speaker says. To avoid this verbal faux pas, a simple pause, more preparation, and practice help. There's power in the pause.

ENGAGE IN VOCAL PRACTICE

During my tenure as a university communication instructor, I use a Shakespeare stanza for a choral reading exercise to warm up students' voices to evaluate and listen to one another. Shakespeare tests pitch, pacing, articulation, and enunciation. Students struggle with the older, British language style, timing their words at a similar pace, and pronouncing the words correctly. They hesitate to project their voices. Instead, students embody nervous vocal and physical delivery. With practice, they moderate their self-judgment of their vocal quality and display their individual personalities. In time, they release the tension, flowing from word to word. Practicing Shakespeare builds vocal confidence.

Express your strongest, most ideal voice and take the time to warm-up, stretch, move up the vocal scale, and change your pace. Hum a favorite tune and hit various consonants and vowels. Articulate lists of words to use each vowel sound. For example, I say fruits: "Watermelon, strawberry, apples, bananas."

How intense should my vocal tone be for this communication context?

Facilitating a creative drama workshop for youth involves louder enthusiastic projection, whereas, presenting a communication workshop to financial planners demands a softer, more deliberative persona and style. What word(s) should I emphasize or inflect my voice to enhance the meaning of the message? Surprising statistics or expressive stories provides opportunities to punch certain words.

POISED PHYSICAL DELIVERY

During a friend's going away party, I meet Elsa, a powerhouse real estate broker, whose strong presence strikes me. With a gallant stride, her stark black hair and focused brown eyes catch my attention. Elsa takes one look at me and declares, "Tina, stand up straighter. Puff your chest out with more confidence." She follows this direct command with, "Let me tell you a story." At ten years old, her mother notices Elsa slouching forward unnaturally and says, "Elsa. I'm reminded of a woman who stood at 4'11" and you wouldn't know it. She stood up with such straight posture, popping her chest forward. She's the definition of confidence. Always stand up straight. You'll feel confident and others around will see you and feel the same energy."

Elsa continues to demonstrate standing upright and encourages me to pose with her. After each attempt, she motivates me to do better, "No, you're still slouching," she says. I'm unaware how much my shoulders hunch forward until Elsa provides this honest and helpful feedback. With consistent diligence, she guides me to have a stronger, poised posture.

You improve your posture by practicing in front of a mirror, walking with a book on your head, and requesting feedback from others. During meetings, make a conscious effort to sit up. Set a timer as a reminder to check your posture. Powerful posture takes awareness, persistence, and feedback.

Poise is a verb.

To feel poised, straighten the shoulders back, press your chest slightly forward, chin up, and gaze straight ahead. Actor Jane

Fonda mentions in a *Wiser Than Me* podcast interview with Julia Louis-Dreyfus the importance of standing up straight in an upright posture expresses bravery and makes you appear younger (Louis-Dreyfus 2023). Theatre professor Gretta Berghammer tells college students to "uncurl your fingers," illustrating speakers can't communicate openly if their body is closed or tense. To lessen hand tension, clench your hands in a fist, holding for five seconds, and then release. Repeat ten times, followed by shaking one hand at a time, counting to ten.

During a workshop session at the 2019 Applied Improvisation Network Conference, facilitator, author of *Playful Mindfulness*, and improviser Ted DesMaisons reveals these insights to help body posture by labeling how we look and feel from a one to a three circle. DesMaisons learns this framework from British acting and vocal coach Patsy Rodenburg:

> Indicating circle "one," the head is looking down and arms are closed. This posture can communicate fear (don't see me) and is hesitant and hiding.

> Demonstrating circle "two" is grounded, upright posture, feet shoulder-width apart, head up, which looks and feels more active, connected, fluid poise-balanced connection.

> Expressing circle "three" includes large gestures, loud vocals, which some receivers fear; it's loud, big, and external—more arrogant ego can overrule.

The difference between each pose is the "two" is open and ready for connection. When I've used this exercise, some participants feel the "one" is physically more comfortable and the "three" difficult to express. Yet, communicating the "two" poses challenges. Being fully seen in front of others increases vulnerability. Posture "two" roots in who you are. In my previous bank job, I reduce my jazzy and enthusiastic "three" persona and choose a relaxed "two" for the audience's comfort.

Meet your audience where they are.

Where do you naturally fall on this spectrum with your body language? What is comfortable for the speaking context?

One = uncomfortable, closed body and softer voice; two = centered-confident voice and body; three = large, loud, big body and voice.

Additionally, move with a purpose. Instead of pacing back and forth, take one oration step forward when sharing an important point or 1-2 steps to the side when transitioning to a new idea or emphasizing a particular word. Movement matters.

In addition to body language, facial expressions matter. I've had clients lament they have a stoic face with recessed eyes. Taller female speakers have expressed they want to be taken seriously. They inquire, "What can I do?" Start with the mindset: think light and soft. Attire creates impact. Wear lighter hues for accessories like scarves or necklaces to compliment darker suits, lean forward toward the audience when speaking, raise the eyebrows, use gentle gestures, softer facial expressions, and speak in a fluid vocal tone. Think and feel lighter; your body will follow.

Finally, eye contact is important. It makes the audience feel as if they are part of the conversation and matter. Divide the audience into three sections and consciously devote similar time to each section. Avoid scanning the audience or looking above their heads. Instead, look into your audience's eyes. Select someone and be with them.

Identify your patterns. Label them, change the pattern, and do the work. Expand your body to demonstrate your internal power. Embody centered-confidence.

Build Your Mental Magnetic, Poised Mindset

Practice tracking your feelings and what your mind, voice, and body are doing. Ask yourself: Is this really the way I want to sound? Look? Be? Am I doing my best? Author Nick Morgan says our body is a punctuation mark and can take charge of our nonverbal communications, projecting the desired, powerful persona in different contexts (2014, 10-12). Our self-awareness, maintaining our magnetic mind, and listening and watching others maximize personal impact. Look in the mirror and balance your head position, body, and loosen your knees. Hold the grounded "two."

Breathe in the "two" and notice your breathing patterns in speaking situations. Are you holding your breath? Is it fast or slower? Breathe from the diaphragm rather than your shoulders or upper body. Keep breathing, pause, and repeat. Like Dory from *Finding Nemo* keeps swimming, magnetic speakers keep breathing, the slower, the better. Repetition creates change. Through consistent work, you're on your way to changing your body's posture.

WEAR YOUR MAGNETIC STYLE

For me, the color purple has always been my favorite color. It's striking and powerful. The color means "communication" and "spiritual." As the top chakra, purple highlights the energy of the work I accomplish with clients. Just like a book has a specific cover and communicates an author's tone and voice, a speaker owns their style. From wearing your logo to donning a striking blazer, put on what feels right and true for the audience and speaking context.

Examine what kind of energy to express, how you take up space, and match your voice and body language. In a networking conversation with stylist Alexandra, I ask her for fashion advice. She says to walk into your closet. Look at your clothing. Breathe and say: "I'm going to put on my power." Decide what attire will get you there. When presenting a keynote, I wear my professional, purple blazer. If I'm facilitating an active, improvisation workshop, I'll change into my black jumpsuit with fun sneakers or comfortable bright-colored clothing for one-on-one client meetings.

Being poised is a choice. Let the purpose guide your message preparation. Be brutally honest with yourself. Thoughts lead to action. Every action or lack of action affects your next move. As Einstein says, "Nothing happens until something moves."

EXERCISES TO ENHANCE
YOUR VOCAL DELIVERY

Think slow; practice your presentation backward, starting with the conclusion and end with the introduction. This practice guides your mind, heart, and voice to focus on the words, the meaning, rather than becoming robotic, moving from line to line. For appropriate breath support, say your presentation lying on the ground.

Think natural. Frame your message as a conversation rather than a performance. Avoid memorizing (unless you're required by TEDx). State your first line, body of the speech, and last line aloud.

Feel positive energy. Go inward. Remember the head is complex, and the heart is simple. Do the preparation, then let the heart lead. Focus on feeling good, and your voice will speak. It's just that simple.

Speak song lyrics aloud varying vocal pace and projection.

EXERCISES TO ENHANCE YOUR PHYSICAL DELIVERY

Divide your space into thirds. Engage in eye contact with each third during a practice.

Let your words guide movement. Avoid thinking, "Am I gesturing enough?" "Should I gesture here?" Your words shape the communication. Trust the words, and your body follows.

Be committed to the space. Whether on stage or in a board room, practice sitting and standing with upright posture. Lift your body and head to show you believe in you.

Stand in front of the mirror, head held high, shoulders back, and feet shoulder-width apart, and state your name with passion and enthusiasm. Fill in the blanks: I am…

Practice the Wonder Woman or victory pose. Place your hands on your hips or hold your arms above your head spread like a "v." Hold two minutes and say your opening line.

Find your Elsa, an accountability partner who provides honest and helpful feedback.

Act "as if," with visuals and props to train your brain to develop muscle memory for the content.

REFLECTION QUESTIONS

Who's an example of a poised communicator I've seen? What qualities did they possess?

How would I describe my vocal style and delivery? Physical delivery?

Would I alter anything with my vocal or physical delivery?

When was a time I felt poised?

How did it feel in my body to be poised?

What steps will I take prior to speaking to be more poised?

What can I practice daily to embody confidence?

MAGNETIC SPEAKERS
FORGIVE OTHERS
AND THEMSELVES

Forgiveness is the attribute of the strong.

—GANDHI

"My father decided to have me killed," Middle Eastern American keynote speaker and leadership consultant Dima Ghawi declares during her Shattering Limitations keynote address. The audience's whispers silence.

In Jordan, years prior, her grandmother holds a transparent, turquoise vase to illustrate the significance of staying perfect, flawless, without cracks, like the vase. Ghawi realizes leaving her husband will dishonor her father and family, yet remaining in an abusive marriage damages her mental and physical health. Eventually, she chooses herself and her well-being and flees to the United States to create a leadership consulting business.

It takes years to grasp she has a story and takes even longer for her to heal from the trauma and gain courage to disclose her heartfelt and painful story. Over time, Ghawi shatters her vase of perfection and opts to forgive herself and others. This intensive inner work allows her to present a magnetic message, with the hope of saving audiences from being crippled by their own perfectionism.

IDENTIFY THE NEED TO FORGIVE

Initially, Ghawi wants to write a book to hide behind printed words, a safer choice than speaking on stage. Each time she speaks, she suffers self-doubt. In 2009, her workaholic lifestyle intensifies, forcing her to stop working and remain on disability for nearly two months.

This break pushes her to take time to think and go through the emotions and shame. The fear and not letting go of her past presses heavy on her heart. Ghawi researches healing methods and reaches out to practitioners to help her heal. During therapy, she recognizes the need to forgive. If she doesn't forgive herself and others, the dense energy continues to weigh down each presentation. Slowly, after years of inner work, she lets in self-love to move forward. Forgiveness gives her power back.

Magnetic speakers forgive.

DEFINING FORGIVENESS

Psychologists define forgiveness as "a conscious, deliberate decision to release feelings of resentment or vengeance toward a person or group who has harmed you, regardless of whether they actually deserve your forgiveness" (Berkley 2023). Additionally, Ryan Howes, PhD, explains forgiveness requires expressing the emotion we're feeling and understanding why we have the need to forgive, let go, and stop ruminating about the past (2009). Instead, we can let in the good feeling energy of enoughness, worthiness, and self-love. Releasing negative feelings toward the self and others strengthens the inner being and empowers the speaker to share their message. This positive shift changes the energetic frequency we and the audience feel.

Dr. Tyler VanderWeele describes two types of forgiveness: decisional and emotional (Harvard Health Publishing 2021). We accomplish decisional forgiveness more quickly and easily, but "emotional forgiveness is much harder and takes longer, as it's common for those feelings to return on a regular basis." The challenge occurs when we remember the memory and suffer from the past event. Lingered suffering heightens negative energy. This energy contributes to continuous negative thoughts and influences a speaker's communication and connection.

Forgiveness is about the other person. Dr. Fred Luskin defines forgiveness as the story the mind creates from the past anger, frustration, or fear (Laurence 2023). Additionally, Robert Enright, PhD, lists three forgiveness factors:

Feeling goodness toward others.

Not being resentful toward the other person.

Offering kindness to the person who hurt you (Laurence 2023).

Forgiveness is a choice, then a feeling. When we forgive, a sense of inner peace evolves, influences our thoughts, feelings, and words. We can learn forgiveness, yet it's hard to forgive ourselves.

FORGIVENESS IS FREEDOM

Psychologist and Holocaust survivor Dr. Edith Eger states one of the proving grounds for freedom is how we relate to our loved ones, take absolute responsibility for our lives, release judgments, and love ourselves as the imperfect, whole human beings we are (2018, 271). Dr. Eger learns a crucial concept from her mother before they part ways at Auschwitz: "Just remember, no one can take away from you what you've put in your mind" (2018, 34). Your thoughts change everything.

It wasn't until a conversation with a friend that I realized my need to forgive a former teacher who called me "Big Mouth" instead of my name. I felt deeply hurt, small, and completely humiliated. My head looked down and my body collapsed in shame for those nine months. This teacher silenced my passionate desire to read aloud, participate, and ask questions in class. Years later, these painful criticisms still shushed me from consistently speaking with sparkling confidence. Forgiveness strengthened my self-love and trust, returning to my enthusiastic identity. Going through the pain and forgiving the judgments I placed on myself and others has reinforced my messages to be more convincing, clear, succinct, and heart-centered. The choice to forgive allows speakers the freedom to express ideas and be the self.

High levels of fear reinforce the inner belief you're broken, thus, impacts feeling free, speaking from the heart (Eger 2022). Ghawi experiences inner freedom by releasing perfectionism.

She grasps the significance of past events, relationships, and view of self and others which affect her communication style. Once she recognizes the deep need to forgive her father, ex-husband, and herself, the healing process transfers into stronger, empowered relationships. Ghawi's internal self-talk compels her to speak and transforms into a dynamic presence: a firm, upright posture and assured, strong vocal authority.

Ghawi says, "To discover the fear of public speaking, what it is, and go deeper and heal it, I paused and asked: 'Why?' 'Why do I feel that fear?' I found I was afraid of disappointing others, which was a similar feeling of disappointing my dad. When I disappointed my dad, there were consequences. Same as if I disappointed an audience. I healed the feelings toward my dad, which impacted my feelings toward an audience." Letting go of the fear and forgiving influences the inner self-talk and manifests a stronger tone and message.

Author Elizabeth Gilbert states, "Walk the speech into your bones" (Forleo 2015). Gilbert notes she's a writer first, speaker second, and explains the audience doesn't need your fear, insecurity, or the questions of self. "Instead," she says, "come into a speaking space with dignity, composure, authority, and complete autonomy. Stand your ground in your female body. Don't be perfect; be finished" (Forleo 2015). When preparing a message, release your inner questioning and desire for perfection. There's no such thing as perfect, just deadlines. Be open and lean into the fear and vulnerability to connect with others. When speakers start with self-forgiveness and self-love, they slowly lessen the need for perfect. Getting good with sharing the self and personal ideas make all the difference.

Magnetic speakers are free.

BENEFITS OF FORGIVENESS AND SELF-COMPASSION
Forgiveness reduces anxiety and depression.

Dr. Kristin Neff defines self-compassion as feeling moved by others' or our suffering (2023). The heart responds with a desire to help and focuses on kindness not judgment. Researcher Kirsten Weir explains, "Forgiveness is linked to mental health outcomes such as reduced anxiety, depression, and major psychiatric disorders" (2017). Additionally, Dr. Enright emphasizes individuals experience less anxiety, more hope, and empowerment when they forgive (Laurence 2023). Being a heart-centered leader and magnetic speaker require taking good care of the mind and physical body. Anxiety affects the body and influences how a speaker creates a message, performs, and relates to others. The more internal stress a speaker carries inside, the more it shows.

Forgiveness increases positive response to acute psychosocial stress (Breines et al. 2014). In this study, researchers train participants to be more self-compassionate. The participants engage in five minutes of loving kindness, meditate for five days, repeat wishes and happiness for the self and others. The self-compassion group shows reduced signs of stress and self-report feeling less anxiety on a stress test. Physiologically, they encounter lower levels of salivary, alpha-amylase (SAA) and a more stable heart rate.

Dr. Neff says, "We tend to treat ourselves harshly when things go wrong" (Long 2017). We can be our worst enemy, contemplating about what's said/not said or someone's reactions to influence future communication and interactions. Dr. Neff emphasizes the importance of stating to yourself, "This is really difficult now. How can I comfort and care for myself in this moment" (Neff 2023)?

During online presentations, I've accidentally hit "mute" or forgotten a visual aid. Instead of self-punishment and scolding, I think, "That happened. Now, what?" I laugh and move forward. I heard of a speaker struggling on stage, referred to notes multiple times, teared up because of these errors. Later, the speaker earns a standing ovation. The audience is more forgiving than you think. Be as compassionate to yourself as your audience is to you.

Self-compassion increases adaptable communication.

One study demonstrates a relationship between adaptive communication behaviors and self-compassion (Long and Neff 2018). Adaptive communication behaviors include asking questions, seeking help, and participating in class. Self-compassionate participants experience reduced anxiety when receiving evaluations and place less value on presenting a certain image to their peers. Their findings suggest individuals who treat themselves more kindly are less concerned with others' judgments and feel more connected. Mindful, compassionate individuals perceive they have less to hide and recognize imperfection as part of the human experience (Long and Neff 2018).

Self-compassion improves communication and connection.

Magnetic speakers are emotionally intelligent. They understand difficult feelings unite us to our common humanity. If we treat ourselves kindly, engage in more compassionate self-talk, we experience better speaking situations. In a study, anxious students prepare a three-minute speech. One group writes about a negative situation at work and the other journals about mindfulness, common humanity, and self-kindness (Harwood and Kocovski 2017). This study discovers those who engage in self-compassion reduce levels of anticipatory anxiety for a speech task and communicate more effectively, whereas, the control group does not experience any improvement. Long explains, "Treating ourselves kindly makes us feel safe and connected, rather than threatened and isolated" (2017).

Self-compassion interconnects sense of self and the belief we're worthy. Even saying kind phrases to ourselves like, "All is well" while resting the hand on our heart expresses self-love. The brain believes these compassionate thoughts. Thus, a speaker will feel differently and present more magnetically.

THE MAGNETIC SPEAKING PROCESS

Being magnetic starts with transforming the mindset and stating internally you have a message worth sharing to others. Following this choice, work inward to heal the deep shame and listen to other's feedback. Through self-acceptance, magnetic speakers trust their ability to speak their truth. Rather than resisting, they're open to receiving help.

Ghawi explains, "I had no idea how to make a message, yet the unwavering passion for influencing people moved me forward to speak." As a form of practice, she starts presenting for free at colleges. She explains, "I was fully horrified of public speaking, crying every time prior, even wishing the taxi taking me to the event would get into an accident on the way." However, following each speech, she acknowledges the high afterward. Ghawi perceives positive feedback from her message's influence, bringing the audience to tears. The powerful impact is too strong to keep her from speaking on stage.

The Process

Decide you have a story/message.

Go through and let go of the shame; forgive yourself and others.

Accept help and trust.

Others can inspire you to speak. Ghawi's friend encourages her to talk about the vase. She says, "I was motivated and more confident because of the extrinsic experience. My confidence didn't come from within; it came from people and trusting them. When I hear my message and see the impact on people, it motivates me to do it more [speaking]." Internal and external motivation to speak generate deeper connections. The desire to speak and practice frequently comes from within. Yet, audience's positive feedback, extrinsic motivation, can encourage future communication.

SPEAKING SERVES OTHERS

Ghawi emphasizes speaking is a service to the audience. Magnetic speakers focus on this service mindset. Our thoughts and ideas support others on their journey, help them grow, learn, and be better human beings. She says, "It's a privilege to be on the stage. Remember that presenting is about serving, helping, inspiring. Ask, 'Why am I doing this?' Remember why you're here. Then be a rebel. I'm a rebel. I change the norms, open doors, getting away from cultural limitations and write a new story."

During one of my communication workshops, a participant explained their discomfort with self-disclosure and preference for working with systems, while their team member identified a desire to go deeper with their colleagues. We discussed the need to help and support one another and acknowledged individual speaking preferences. To see the other and be in an attitude of service builds connection with your team and influences conversations in a powerful way.

Ghawi explains, "To get over the fear, keep doing it [speaking]. It's that simple. Keep presenting ideas and speaking. Get on the stage. I'd cry, and then get on the stage. I thought about getting a full-time job and quit speaking, but the *impact on others was too strong*. I needed to go through it [speaking], so I can understand my audience's pain and purpose. That's how you make a difference, for it's something much bigger than us." Magnetism requires being open to the speaking journey, receive help to uplevel individual speaker style, serve others, and express vulnerability. The fear softens when we serve others. And, in your own way, be a rebel; change norms for the greater good.

When you focus on serving your audience, your message makes long-lasting impacts.

TINA'S TIPS TO FORGIVE AND BE MAGNETIC

Practice writing and saying heart-centered gratitudes aloud. These proclamations place the head and heart in a place to present with more punch and power.

Feel the feelings, then move forward to a service focus.

Have a consistent spiritual practice.

Empathize with others to comprehend their experience.

Be realistic with how you feel about speaking. For Dima, she scored her public speaking fear a twenty-seven out of ten; her fear was deep. Know your starting point to begin the work.

EXERCISE

Stephanie Albright, intuitive and spiritual guide says, "Be present. Be silent. Listen for three things. Label them. Then six. Then ten. Before you know it, you'll hear your heartbeat. This helps you align with your heart and your presence." The goal is to get closer to the reality of what is and let go of the past or future fear stories, a compassionate, forgiving place.

Quiet your mind chatter.

Be aware of your triggers.

Focus your attention on the feeling you desire.

Develop, think, write, and say powerful statements to yourself prior to communicating. Before each presentation I say the following statement: "I'm a passionate, connected, and confident speaker. I love myself and am whole, enough, and complete."

REFLECTION QUESTIONS

Who do I need to forgive?

Do I trust others? Why or why not? How do people gain my trust? What are my expectations?

What am I thinking and feeling prior to speaking? Is what I'm thinking and feeling where I want to be?

"Fears kept hidden only grow more fierce. Habits worse" (Eger 2022). List your fears. When it comes to speaking in front of others, what am I afraid of? Why?

What habits am I doing currently? What habits can I start doing to improve my self-love and compassion?

What will I do daily to expand my magnetic speaker style?

THE PRACTICE: DO THE WORK

---

*It's freeing when you present your ideas with honor,
and rigorous, focused practice will get you there.*

—TINA B.

Staring at thirty women's faces on Zoom, my business coach says with affectionate warmth, "Tina, you need to perform a visibility challenge on Facebook. You're struggling with promoting your business on camera."

Each time I stare into the computer screen, my breath comes in shallow gasps, my chest heavy, weighted with fear, as my heart hammers a thunderous beat against my ribcage. This video resistance persists. What issues do I have with speaking on camera? Why invest time and effort on social media? Will anybody listen or care? During this coaching call, my body squirms at the thought of presenting online, and I don't know why.

My business coach observes my lengthy, hesitant vocal pauses and blank, glazed-over eyes as I freeze with each online coaching call. As an emotional, type-A over-achiever, I've always battled perfection, punishing myself if a task doesn't meet unrealistic expectations. Even perfection prevents starting a business for more than a decade. From earning the best grades to pleasing people, now, perfectionism leaks into my communication style.

Day one of the visibility challenge: I question what I'm saying, how I'm saying it, and how I look. Stiff posture and arm pits dripping with perspiration, immobilized, I fail to hit record. My normal cheery, energetic disposition morphs into a depleted, empty shell. Stuck in a spiral of analysis paralysis, hands shaking, I slowly click "Live" to not let my coach down. Day by day, my tight, taut voice squeaks words into a tiny cell phone screen to hide my intense self-doubt and fear.

Magnetic speakers show up and practice.

AUDIENCE-CENTERED COMMUNICATION
REQUIRES INTRINSIC MOTIVATION

This visibility challenge forces the exploration into inner confidence. Speakers must tune inward for inspiration, envision positive audience reactions, and create a conversation. In Richard Greene's TEDx Talk, he addresses the difference among styles of performance, presentation, and conversation (Greene 2014). This distinction is in the pronoun: performers speak *at* their audience; presenters speak *to* their audience; and conversationists speak *with* their audience.

While theatre and performance background skills help, they can create a hindrance. It's easy to evolve into "performer" mode with meticulous precision and heightened fastidiousness. I long to portray a professional and proficient Tina B. speaking consultant image. Virtual communication alters my conversational style. Speaking into a screen, not seeing or feeling people's energy, exhausts and depletes me. Each day, this experiment provides a wild awareness of wrestling to anchor in my confidence.

By day twenty-six, my mindset shifts. Like a caterpillar experiences a metamorphosis, I transform. Standing upright, arms lightly at my side, chin forward, my firm, strong voice echoes a message fluidly and deliberately as the minutes pass. Initially, the idea of speaking on screen without viewing and sensing audience energy triggers negative, judgmental thoughts. I expand into a growth mindset.

One study shows a growth mindset associates less public speaking anxiety in a classroom setting (Stewart et al. 2019). Researchers find if a participant's mindset remains stable, speaking anxiety decreases and self-perceived speaking competence significantly increases from the beginning to the end of class. Additionally, participants develop "more sophisticated beliefs about public speaking as an expressive, transformational, and audience-centric endeavor" (Stewart et al. 2019).

Each day, I commit to appear on screen no matter what, sharing an idea. Finally, the perfectionism of "looking good" and "getting it right" wanes. Instead of letting go of perfectionism, I learn to work with and through it as my authentic self returns.

During this thirty-day visibility challenge, I experience a magnificent awakening: I care more than my audience cares about the "look" of the video. The love and enthusiasm of sharing an idea shapes the message and softens the fear. My business coach checks in and asks, "How are you feeling with the process and your progress?" Repeating a scary skill equates fewer fearful thoughts and heightened successful speaking. Online videos emerge into a routine.

To be magnetic, speakers must be intrinsically motivated, let the passion for the topic and care to serve others motivate their communication, instead of the selfish wish of looking good and being perfect. Releasing judgments takes more than mindset. It takes awareness and practice. Lots and lots of practice. To transform into a beautiful butterfly, connection with others comes from within. Being aware of inner self-talk and embracing who you are makes you more magnetic.

Even with practice, speech anxiety can exist.

SPEAKING APPREHENSION DEFINED

Communication researcher Dr. Karen Dwyer defines communication apprehension as "fear or anxiety associated with real or anticipated communication with others" (Dwyer 1998, 9). Speaking anxiety comes in many forms, from sweaty palms to blushing, to muscle tension or shortness of breath (Lawrenz and Montijo 2022). Dr. Dwyer stresses the key to speaking success requires the speaker's commitment to improve, actively learning the skill, practicing, and participating in opportunities to overcome stage fright in different communication circumstances (Dwyer 1998, 4). These factors are all in our control, however, some speaking apprehension is innate.

Researcher Hemantha Kottawatta conducts a study with 686 high school students, noting the Big Five Personality Traits of extroversion, openness to experience, agreeableness, and conscientiousness have a positive and significant influence when communicating (2019). Extroverts who are more open, agreeable, and conscientious experience higher levels of expressiveness and precision when they communicate. Additionally, Kottawatta also finds neuroticism has a strong impact with verbal aggressiveness, emotionality, and manipulative styles of communication (2019). Thus, certain innate personality traits directly correlate with having less anxiety, an increased willingness to speak, and use appropriate communication in given contexts.

In addition to the previous study, researcher Kim Jin-Young explores the level of extroversion and openness in personality affects speech performance and the situational factor of the amount of rehearsal influences the level of communication apprehension (2015). While some have personality traits with an increased desire to speak, the speaker's commitment to learning and practicing the skill is what matters. Making the conscious choice, having consistent practice, and doing the work increase confidence.

Both self-proclaimed introverts Mary Swander and Andrew Tarvin express their speaking success and lowered communication apprehension has developed from consistent practice of the skill over time. While Swander finds dressing up as a character and acting "as if" increases her confidence, Tarvin uses improvisation training and stand-up comedy to stretch his abilities and temper any speaking anxiety.

YOUR PERSPECTIVE LESSENS THE FEAR

Singer and keynote performer Stephanie Bonte-Lebair discusses magnetic speakers create a clear intention to connect with their content. Singing has made her love speaking and brings comfort, plus performing repeatedly and staying consistent with her process increases confidence. Developing a centered and comfortable foundation, a speaker ritual, is essential. Bonte-Lebair reflects on her process and performance and is willing to do different based on feedback.

Bonte-Lebair explains overcoming stage fright. She says, "As a musician and performer, I get stage fright. I don't eliminate the fear. I've learned to manage and transform that energy, so it works for or with me, not against me." In graduate school, Bonte-Lebair sings the difficult main role Rosalinda in the opera *Die Fledermaus*. One night, something doesn't feel right. She starts singing the aria and notices a tightness in her throat. As her throat closes, she barely hits the high notes. Bonte-Lebair's panic swells as she approaches the hardest part of the song.

"I saw the other actors on stage with big, wide eyes as if to say, 'Oh, my goodness, I don't know what's happening to you.' I'm freaking out. True to the vision I had created for myself, I didn't get the last note. I was so embarrassed."

The next night, she has to perform again. Determined to show the cast she has what it takes to perform a leading role, Bonte-Lebair creates a completely different outcome. Rich and pure, her voice belts out the aria better than she's ever sung, holding the high note one second longer than the orchestra.

Bonte-Lebair says, "What caused me to fail one night, only to triumph the next? The difference between night one and night two wasn't my talent. It was how I perceived my fear. *The difference between fear and excitement is simply your perspective.*" Bonte-Lebair's mindset modification, her consistent practice, and thorough evaluation improved future performances. Magnetism comes from the act of getting up and doing the performance again. And again. And again.

Mindset Develops Your Magnetic Speaker Style

Keynote speaker and leadership executive coach Sarah Noll Wilson explains the importance of calming your amygdala, which affects communication (2022, 44-48). This part of the brain becomes overstimulated and triggers an individual into fight or flight. Wilson provides three steps to work through the stress and lessen anxiety:

Notice and name. What's triggering you? What's causing the fear?

Technology and virtual presentations can cause worry. What if the technology doesn't work when needed? Release the fear by first acknowledging it. Do you worry your car won't start every time you turn the key in the ignition? Translate that assuredness to showing up online. Just trust the computer will work and the right people will listen. This attitude shift changes everything.

Breathe.

After labeling the fear, take control of the breath. Listen to your breathing patterns. Is your pace rapid? Slow down. Pause and release the exhale steadily to calm the body and mind.

Take a break.

Make space for the mind and body. Prior to speaking, go to the restroom, walk outdoors, or get a drink of water, anything to focus and change to a present and confident mindset (Wilson 2022, 51-57).

Additionally, Wilson emphasizes the importance of getting curious with the self and others. Being results-driven requires questioning if your reaction is a preference, process, or performance (Wilson 2022, 122). Humans have a bias toward negative thoughts; therefore, work toward positive thoughts and feelings. Trusting the self and being open and curious moves you forward.

BE MOTIVATED TO PRACTICE CONTENT AND DELIVERY
Magnetic speakers engage in concentrated, consistent practice over a long period of time and receive guided feedback from a coach. Communication Studies Professor Dr. Marty Birkholt says, "Practice and coaching go hand in hand. It's asking two questions: How quickly do you want to get there, and how good do you want to be?"

Dr. Birkholt has coached several college students and consulted multiple professionals with their vocal and physical delivery. We discuss the ten thousand hours rule to achieve true expertise in a skill, which Birkholt says is a weird rule.

It's an arbitrary number, closer to what international, professional pianist Joyce Yang will achieve as she practices between six-eight hours daily, resting only one day a month.

Dr. Birkholt works with individuals who demonstrate what he calls "abysmal gestures." He explains it takes one thousand repetitions for their gestures to become natural. He notes, "It depends on where they start and where they want to go." Supporting Birkholt's concept coaching improves speaking skills, a study uncovers psychological and behavioral interventions with a therapist in person or virtually reduce the fear of public speaking (Ebrahimi et al. 2019). Their research indicates participants continue to improve using the learned strategies after treatment.

Additionally, Dr. Birkholt describes the difference between practice quality and quantity. Number of repetitions matters. "Shorter practices and more frequently is most effective. Three hours over six days is better than three hours in one day. Most individuals can't maintain a high-level focus for an extended period of time; one hour max for practice time on presentation skills." Dr. Birkholt shares an example of a client who wants to soften his accent. When his client only practices during coaching sessions, the rate of improvement drops dramatically. The client needs intrinsic motivation and commitment to practice. Dr. Birkholt says, "Experts can give specific areas to improve and how to focus. Just like only playing basketball doesn't make you better, you need the directed coaching to get better faster." To be magnetic entails choices: a strong work ethic, thoughtful, guided practice, and consistent repetition over shorter blocks of time with the feedback loop to improve.

Furthermore, magnetic speakers learn to be more inclusive and interactive from speaking more. In a study, researchers explain improvement happens from practicing in conversation, composition, and delivery skills (O'Hair, Stewart, and Rubenstein 2012). Author Scott Kaufman states, "Another way individual differences [in performance] matter is by sustaining the motivation to practice over an extended period of time. While deliberate practice is important (no one denies that), it's no easy feat to sustain that practice over the long haul and just *keep showing up*" (2014). Several of my clients abstain from saying their speech aloud during rehearsals. Presenters who flail on stage clearly fail to take practicing seriously. Perhaps they think, "I've got this," or "I've looked at my note cards, and that's good enough." It's not.

My son selects Scott Joplin's piano piece "Rag Time" to play. Initially, he expects to "get it" quickly and effortlessly. Eventually, he alters his expectations, listens to a professional play the selection online, trains his ears to the cadence and tone, and devotes time each day to practice. His commitment to daily rehearsal in different ways, slow, fast, and measures in varied order, leads him to his ultimate goal: memorizing the piece. By setting a clear, achievable goal, with the right amount of challenge, my son finds joy in the practice.

Speaking magnetically takes focused effort: Do the Work.

Client, farmer, and owner of Pinoak Farm, Seth, works to develop and practice his TEDx Talk. Seth has never memorized a talk before, and his lips become firm and his voice thickens when he explains his nervousness. He says, "The TEDx experience was a confidence booster. It taught me what I was capable of. I learned this is how hard you've got to work and take speaking seriously. When I've listened to others, I've learned how little people have communication training." Magnetic speakers don't wing it. They prepare and practice with intention.

TINA'S TEDX SPEAKING TIPS:
Be dedicated to practice daily.

Be strategic and selective in finding the right people to give clear, focused feedback prior.

Practice in a variety of ways: task-completion, self-recording, and with friends and family.

Psychologist Dr. Kim Hoogeveen says, "I've been told people like to read what I write. What they don't see is I rewrote a page of text five times and spent 1.5 hours making careful changes. Sometimes I've been told by others they wish they could write like me. Often, I think they likely could if they're willing to put in the work. The same goes for speaking. When you invest the time to create great content, you are 70 percent of the way home to a great presentation. When you spend the time to make the presentation strong—all the way from your performance skills to the audio-visual aspects—you will find your confidence soars and your anxiety fades."

Magnetic speaking demands the choice to do the work, stay committed, and then see and feel results. Be intentional with when and how often you practice. Practice often on your own and in front of people. *Practice period.*

OVERCOMING RESISTANCE TO PRACTICE

We can, however, feel resistance to rehearse. Author Steven Pressfield emphasizes resistance to any creative work or craft is the enemy and difficult to defeat (2002, 7). While resistance can't be seen, touched, heard, or smelled, we feel it. Facilitating a meeting or creating an engaging presentation can be demanding. What can hold a speaker back are the three "p's": procrastination, perfectionism, and paralysis from analysis (Blount 2023). This deep, energetic force repels us from doing the work. We get distracted. We procrastinate, filling our space with anything but the work. Disrupt the three "p's" and lean into your creative craft.

Instead of becoming a victim or allowing the ego to take over, evoke your creative muse. Creativity author Julia Cameron provides twelve weeks of activities and guidance in her book *The Artist's Way: A Spiritual Path to Higher Creativity* (2016). She explains initiating your creative spirit involves choosing to be creative. Cameron includes three basic practices: View yourself as creative and develop and say aloud affirmations; compose three judgment-free pages daily in a journal; and participate in weekly solo, artist dates, which may include visiting an art gallery, taking a walk, or coloring or painting (2016, 11-24). The ultimate goal is to discover your creative identity, then practice.

Committing to do the work involves a mindset shift. Your message isn't just about you. The shift from "I" to "we" tempers resistance. Construct your message to serve the audience. Keynote speaker, Dima Ghawi says, "It's knowing your talk is no longer about you. It's about your audience. Shift your perception, for you're here to serve. Open your mind and give

permission to let go of stuck. Have persistence, not patience."
Persistence, and as Pressfield calls being a "pro," acknowledges
what you're doing isn't art; it's a craft (2002, 69-70). Crafting
a magnetic message takes pushing through the resistance.
Resistance is something you go through not sit in.

PRACTICE VISUAL IMAGERY

Laurel Parnell, PhD, explains to use our creative imagination to
calm anxiety and lessen speaking apprehension through visualizing a safe place, tapping into nurturing and wise figures, and
acting "as if" (2008, 135-141). We have inner natural resources
to discover peace in the moment, embrace the audience, and
step into a confident mindset. Parnell notes our sense of self is
based on our interpretations of our experience. If we imagine
we're engaged in an activity, the brain neurons are activated
as if we're actually doing it (Parnell 2008, 28). Practicing prior,
wearing empowering attire, feeling the "as if"-ness, and owning
our energy and space translate to future powerful presentations.

Inner peace comes from being in the knowing of the topic
and your ability. Prior to a university interview, I envision
standing in the classroom, teaching college students. For
one month, I picture wearing my black blazer and providing
guidance and feedback on student speeches. This experience
lets my heart lead the reality. My brain motivates to believe
this truth, and later, I receive the job offer.

Speakers work with the positive feeling and build the inner
strength. Be in a place of joy, lightness, and love, a friend to the self.

Magnetic speakers see, feel, and trust themselves and their audience.

EXERCISE 1

Conduct a visibility challenge. Select a social media platform (Facebook, LinkedIn, YouTube, etc.) and present a daily video for thirty days. You'll break the habit of thinking "Can I?" to "I can!"

EXERCISE 2

Create a speaker ritual. A speaker ritual includes behaviors and thoughts the day, hours, and minutes prior to a speaking engagement or meeting. Get into the speaker zone, have a clear, positive, concentrated focus. Avoid cramming last minute. Distractions lead to disjointed communication.

Prompts to Create a Speaker Ritual

Fuel your mind.

Create spaciousness devoted to writing an audience-centered message. Provide quiet time for yourself. Sit in silence and close your eyes. Envision yourself in the speaking space. What does it look like? Sound like? Feel like? Picture the audience reacting positively to your words. Tune into this energy. Where are you feeling joy in your body? Thoughts create words; words generate actions and behaviors, which determine our being.

Fuel your voice.

Prepare and practice your talk aloud in your authentic self in various ways: walk your dog, converse with friends and family, say it in your office or car. Train your brain to feel the words and land the message in the hearts of your audience.

Fuel your body.

Have a morning ritual and focus on appropriate food intake and movement. Eat a light breakfast. Avoid dairy, caffeine, high fat and high sugar foods. Move your body. Do yoga poses, stretches, walk, and/or dance to invigorate the body.

Fuel your soul.

To cleanse your mind, breathe slowly in through the nose and out through the nose, seven breaths, pausing for seven seconds, and releasing for seven. To lessen anxiety in your body, breathe in through the nose and out through the mouth. Don't forget to breathe prior, during, and after communicating. Slowing your breath centers you.

EXERCISE 3

Conduct an "as if" practice with visual aids and in wearing your attire.

Rehearse your speech days prior then trust yourself.

REFLECTION QUESTIONS

How do I feel prior to presenting an idea? During? After?

When do I experience fear with speaking? What level?

How often do I practice?

How will I overcome resistance to rehearsing?

What's my speaker ritual? The day prior? The day of? Following the presentation?

What can I start doing prior to speaking to ensure a powerful connection with my audience?

How will I see, feel, and trust myself to be the magnetic speaker I am?

TINA'S FINAL WORD...

Dear Magnetic Speaker,

What's your inner self-talk tape playing? Are you compassionate and trusting or cluttering your mind with insecurities, fearful of the future? Your creative brain can compose an anxious story and create realistic characters and setting, exacerbating those emotions to affect your performance. Ask yourself, what's the worst possible thing to happen? Sit with this thought for only a minute. Then, say, "Be gone!" and let the limiting thought go. Let in the present moment, the "who" that you are.

Now, picture yourself in the space. Breathe slowly, pausing in between breaths. Envision yourself doing well. What are you seeing? What are you saying aloud? Feel centered-confidence and say your first line. Picture audience faces reacting with the outcome you desire. What are you feeling? Where are you feeling it?

Vocalize your message. Go with heart. What feels true and natural to you?

Do what's most comfortable and aligns with your message, speaker style, and purpose. Practice with and without your notes, walking indoors and out. Act "as if" with props, visual aids, attire, and trust yourself. Do the work. Feel the words. Be in your being.

Like a budding rose, grow, share your beauty, and give yourself compassion. Be full of humanity.

May you anchor into your authentic style and confidence and create the desired impact. You are magnetic!

Sincerely,
Tina B. your Communication Consultant and Coach

ACKNOWLEDGMENTS

———

When I started this journey, I had no idea just how difficult it would be. The mental strain of balancing and juggling the responsibilities of running my business with my family and personal life, along with the physical exhaustion and slog of hours of research, interviewing, writing, editing, and editing more, were the biggest challenges I've encountered in my life. Not to mention the emotional highs and lows and feeling the sheer vulnerability as I discovered my writer's voice. "Trust the process" became the hardest and at times, most frustrating phrase to embrace. And yet, it's the most empowering one, for all I've learned and how much I've grown from writing this book.

I didn't accomplish this book alone. Throughout my entire journey, I've had an incredible group of dedicated humans to support this invigorating and tiring voyage.

First, to my book backers: Thank you for purchasing my book prior to printing.

Jon Bakehouse, Stacey Clark, Jeanne-Marie Bakehouse, Ryan Reed, Marcea Seible, Andrea Woodward, Amy Palma, Mary

Sand, Nancy Bakehouse, Bruce Leslie, Yvonne Silver, Brian Aust, Jeff Dentlinger, Caroline Gillissen, Nina and Larry Carley, Larry Brandstetter, Emerson Bostrom, Kat Parent, Deb Crowe, Clint Clark, Nancy Buller, Cynthia Shelton, Dena Synder, Jenny Marburger, Kris Scharingson, Predrag Kopun, Patricia Sullivan, Lora Kaup, Alex Pearson, Mary P Lynch, Karen Eischeid, Jim Manning, Ivy Woolf Turk, Sophia Mego, Mom and Dad, Chad Williams, Kathy Muzik, Nancy Rowe, Mike Rowe, Linda Marshall, Tomara Moss, Eric Koester, Megan Gillespie

To my wise and interesting interviewees: Thank you for taking the time to share your knowledge and expertise with me. Oh, how much I learned from you and the rich, deep conversations about what it means to be magnetic from various perspectives.

AlexSandra Leslie, Amber Howard, Andrew Tarvin, Andy Mort, Brian Drury, Darcy Maulsby, Dr. Deanne Gute, Dima Ghawi, Elvira Marie Chang, Erik Dominguez, Erin Duffy, Dr. Gary Gute, Frank King, Gretta Berghammer, Ivy Woolf Turk, Dr. John McKenna, Jude Treder-Wolff, Dr. Kim Hoogeveen, Dr. Marty Birkholt, Mary Swander, Sarah Archer, Stephanie Bontair-Lebair

For impactful conversations that made the book–Sonia Cuvelier-Walsh, Stacey Clark,Ted Barr, Michael Marvosh, Heather McMillian, Elsa de Sousa, Dr. Caryn Willens, and Shelley Riutta

To my clients–Seth, Meg, Cynthia, Heather, Tony, Cole, Katie: Thank you for your willingness to share your stories and have them in print.

To my beta readers for all the helpful feedback and questions to assist in my editing process.

Betty Johnston, Bruce Leslie, Dr. Delann Soenksen, Dena Synder, Jeanne-Marie Bakehouse, Lila Hoogeveen, Lora Kaup, Dr. Marcea Seible, Mom and Dad, Nancy Bakehouse

To the Manuscript team and editors: Thank you for all the assistance in developing, structuring, and revising to help me create a better, stronger book.

To Gjorgji Pejkovski and his design team for developing my book cover.

To my amazing marketing strategist Jacques Moolman for your calm, gentle kindness to guide me through the book marketing process. You encouraged me, made me laugh when I needed it most, and worked hard to assist me in creating my very first promotional video with B-roll. You are beyond valuable.

To Nausheen Bari, Cheri Gipson, and Jessica Koch's marketing team: Thank you for assisting me with crafting newsletters and social media posts to inform others about my book's progress and promote events.

To Mom and Dad, for the supportive phone calls, handwritten notes, and even a yummy bag of homemade gooey caramel corn for comfort. I appreciate you asking me how I'm doing, expressing how proud you are, and celebrating this accomplishment. I love you both!

To my other family members and friends for your calls, conversations, and notes of encouragement.

To my son: Thank you for reminding me to play, take breaks, and for being patient when I had to bury myself into hours of writing in my office. I love how much you believe in me, saying my book will be a best seller. Thank you for dreaming big and encouraging me to dream big. I love you so.

And, to Jon, my loving partner and best friend. Thank you for the early morning coffee talks, rich questions, and unconditional support, from composing encouraging notes, giving out comforting hugs, and saying what I needed to hear to push me through the hardest of times. Thank you for quieting my sabotaging thoughts, encouraging me to keep going, and believing in me, knowing I'd write a book. I'm forever grateful for your grounded, calm spirit, and encouragement and love. We're lucky. Love you.

Thank you to all the readers who choose to read this book and share their heart-centered message to the world to make positive changes. You are magnetic!

APPENDIX

INTRODUCTION

Coleman, John. 2014. "A Speech is Not an Essay." *Business Communication* (blog), *Harvard Business Review*. September 11, 2014. https://hbr.org/2014/09/a-speech-is-not-an-essay.

Duarte Inc. 2023. "The Duarte Method." Duarte. Accessed January 11, 2023. https://www.duarte.com/approach/duarte-method/.

Gallo, Carmine. 2014. "New Survey: 70% Say Presentation Skills Are Critical for Career Success." *Forbes Leadership Strategy* (blog), *Forbes*. September 25, 2014. https://www.forbes.com/sites/carminegallo/2014/09/25/new-survey-70-percent-say-presentation-skills-critical-for-career-success/?sh=5d39821e8890.

Nelson, Leigh C., Toni S. Whitfield, and Michelle Moreau. 2012. "I Need Help: Help Seeking Behaviors, Communication Anxiety and Communication Center Usage." *Basic Communication Course Annual* 24, no. 10: 151-180. https://core.ac.uk/reader/232829530.

Raja, Farhan. 2017. "Anxiety Level in Students of Public Speaking: Causes and Remedies." *Journal of Education and Educational Development* 4, no. 1 (June): 94-107. https://files.eric.ed.gov/fulltext/EJ1161521.pdf.

Ruiz, Don. 1997. *The Four Agreements: A Practical Guide to Personal Freedom*. San Rafael, CA: Amber-Allen Publishing Inc.

Zauderer, Steven. 2023. "31 Fear of Public Speaking Statistics." *Cross River Therapy*. January 11, 2023. https://www.crossrivertherapy.com/public-speaking-statistics.

WHAT DOES IT MEAN TO BE A MAGNETIC SPEAKER?

Antonakis, John, Marika Fenley, and Sue Liechti. 2012. "Learning Charisma." *Leadership Development* (blog), *Harvard Business Review*. June 2012. https://hbr.org/2012/06/learning-charisma-2.

Antonakis, John. 2015. "Let's Face it: Charisma Matters." TEDx Talks. March 18, 2015. 16:03. https://www.youtube.com/watch?v=SEDvD1IICfE.

Brown, Brené. 2014. "How to Be Yourself, Even in Life's Most Anxiety-Inducing Moments." *O, The Oprah Magazine*, August 2014. https://www.oprah.com/spirit/brene-brown-advice-how-to-be-yourself/2.

Duarte, Nancy. 2012. "The Secret Structure of Great Talks." TED Talks. February 5, 2012. 18:01. https://www.ted.com/talks/nancy_duarte_the_secret_structure_of_great_talks?language=en.

Goldberg, Briar. 2019. "Before Your Next Presentation or Speech, Here's the First Thing You Must Think About." *Business* (blog), *Ideas.TED.com*. October 29, 2019. https://ideas.ted.com/before-your-next-presentation-or-speech-heres-the-first-thing-you-must-think-about/.

Oxford Reference. 2023. "Charisma." *Oxford University Press*. 2023. Accessed June 6, 2023. https://www.oxfordreference.com/display/10.1093/oi/authority.20110803095603124;jsessionid=CFB2E8D13938E7AF521BB6BA54FF86A8.

THE WHO THAT WE ARE: OUR SOULS SPEAK

American Psychological Association. 2023. "Self-concept." *APA Dictionary of Psychology*. 2023. Accessed June 6, 2023. https://dictionary.apa.org/self-concept.

Anderson, John R. 2020. *Cognitive Psychology and Its Implications*, 9th ed. New York, NY: Worth Publishers MacMillan Learning.

Chopra, Deepak. 2010. *Reinventing the Body, Resurrecting the Soul: How to Create a New You*. New York, NY: Harmony.

Chopra, Deepak. 1994. "Chapter 1: Law of Pure Potentiality." *The Seven Spiritual Laws of Success: A Practical Guide to the Fulfillment of Your Dreams*. Novato, CA: New World Library.

Coelho, Paulo. 1995. *The Alchemist*. London, England: Thorsons.

Cuddy, Amy. 2015. *Presence: Bringing Your Boldest Self to Your Biggest Challenges*. New York, NY: Hachette Book Company.

Eurich, Tasha. 2018. "What Self-Awareness Really Is (and How to Cultivate It)." *Emotional Intelligence* (blog), *Harvard Business Review*. January 4, 2018. https://hbr.org/2018/01/what-self-awareness-really-is-and-how-to-cultivate-it.

Katie, Byron. 2023. "The Work is a Practice." *The Work of Byron Katie*. Accessed February 1, 2023. https://thework.com/instruction-the-work-byron-katie/.

Kolb, Bryan, Ian Q. Whishaw, and G. Campbell Teskey. 2019. *An Introduction to Brain and Behavior*, 6th ed. New York, NY: Worth Publishers MacMillan Learning.

Lenard-Cook, Lisa. 2008. *The Mind of Your Story: Discover What Drives Your Fiction.* Cincinnati, OH: Reader's Digest Books.

Li, Tingting, Tongtong Jiang, Genya Shi, Chunli Song, and Tieying Shi. 2022. "Correlation Between Self-Awareness, Communication Ability and Caring Ability of Undergraduate Nursing Students: A Cross-Sectional Study." *Nurse Education Today* 116, (September). https://doi.org/10.1016/j.nedt.2022.105450.

McLeod, Saul. 2023. "Freud's Theory of Personality: Id, Ego, and Superego." *Theories: Freudian Psychology* (blog), *Simply Psychology.* February 20, 2023. https://simplypsychology.org/psyche.html.

Medical News Today. 2020. "Left Brain vs. Right Brain: Fact and Fiction." Healthline Media. March 16-20, 2020. Accessed February 1, 2023. https://www.medicalnewstoday.com/articles/321037.

McMahan, Ian. 2019. "The Power of Your Subconscious Mind Summary and Review." Review of *The Power of Your Subconscious* by Joseph Murphy. https://lifeclub.org/books/the-power-of-your-subconscious-mind-joseph-murphy-ian-mcmahan-revised-review-summary.

Nemeth, Maria. 2023. "You Have Inner Gold–Part One: The Dilemma." *Dr. Maria Nemeth Blog* (blog). February 2, 2023. https://marianemeth.com/inner-gold/.

Nielsen, Jared A., Brandon A. Zielinski, Michael A. Ferguson, Janet E. Lainhart, and Jeffrey S. Anderson. 2013. "An Evaluation of the Left-Brain vs. Right-Brain Hypothesis with Resting State Functional Connectivity Magnetic Resonance Imaging." *PLOS ONE* 8, no. 8 (August): e71275. https://doi.org/10.1371/journal.pone.0071275.

Powell, Russell A., Lynne P. Honey, and Diane G. Symbaluk. 2017. *Introduction to Learning and Behavior,* 5th ed. Australia: Cengage Learning.

Sutton, Anne. 2016. "Measuring the Effects of Self-Awareness: Construction of the Self-Awareness Outcomes Questionnaire." *Europe's Journal of Psychology* 12, no. 4 (November): 645-658. https://doi.org/10.5964/ejop.v12i4.1178.

OWNING YOUR MAGNETIC PERSONALITY

Duarte Inc. 2023. "The Duarte Method." Duarte. Accessed January 11, 2023. https://www.duarte.com/approach/duarte-method/.

Hopwood, Christopher J., M. Brent Donnellan, Daniel M. Blonigen, Robert F. Krueger, Matt McGue, William G. Iacono, and S. Alexandra Burt. 2011. "Genetic and Environmental Influences on Personality Trait Stability and Growth During the Transition to Adulthood: A Three-Wave Longitudinal Study." *Journal of Personality and Social Psychology* 100, no. 3 (March): 545-56. https://psycnet.apa.org/doi/10.1037/a0022409.

Keirsey, David. 1998. *Please Understand Me II: Temperament, Character, Intelligence.* Del Mar, CA: Prometheus Nemesis Book Company.

Lim, Annabelle. 2023. "Big Five Personality Traits: The 5-Factor Model of Personality." *Theories: Personality* (blog), *Simply Psychology*. February 8, 2023. https://simplypsychology.org/big-five-personality.html.

Little, Brian. 2016. "Who are You, Really? The Puzzle of Personality." TEDx Talks. October 14, 2016. 18:21. https://www.youtube.com/watch?v=NZ509PcHeL0.

Kuntze, Jeroen, Henk T. van der Molen, and Marise Ph. Born. 2016. "Big Five Personality Traits and Assertiveness do not Affect Mastery of Communication Skills." *Health Professions Education* 2, no. 1 (June): 33-43. https://doi.org/10.1016/j.hpe.2016.01.009.

Mitchell, Kevin. 2022. "How much of our personality is innate?" *The Genetics Society Podcast*. Released July 12, 2022. 34 min. https://geneticsunzipped.com/transcripts/2022/7/14/kevin-mitchell-innate.

National Library of Medicine. 2022. "Is Temperament Determined by Genetics?" *Medline Plus*. July 12, 2022. https://medlineplus.gov/genetics/understanding/traits/temperament.

Power, R.A., and M. Pluess. 2015. "Heritability Estimates of the Big Five Personality Traits Based on Common Genetic Variants." *Translational Psychiatry* 5, no. 7 (July): e604. https://doi.org/10.1038/tp.2015.96.

Sims, Ceri M. 2016. "Do the Big-Five Personality Traits Predict Empathic Listening and Assertive Communication?" *International Journal of Listening* 31, no. 3. (July): 162-188. https://doi.org/10.1080/10904018.2016.1202770.

MAGNETIC SPEAKERS ARE AUTHENTIC

Bach, Richard. 2014. *Jonathan Livingston Seagull: A Story. The Complete Edition.* London, UK: Harper Thorsons.

Cuddy, Amy. 2012. "Your Body Language May Shape Who You Are." TED. June 25, 2012. 20:46. https://www.ted.com/talks/amy_cuddy_your_body_language_may_shape_who_you_are/c.

Copeland, William E., Lilly Shanahan, Jennifer Hinesley, Robin F. Chan, Karolina A. Aberg, John A. Fairbank, Edwin J. C. G. van den Oord, and E. Jane Costello. 2018. "Association of Childhood Trauma Exposure with Adult Psychiatric Disorders and Functional Outcomes." *JAMA Network Open* 1, no. 7 (November): e184493. https://jamanetwork.com/journals/jamanetworkopen/fullarticle/2713038.

Eurich, Tasha. 2018. "The Right Way to Respond to Negative Feedback." *Difficult Conversations* (blog), *Harvard Business Review*. May 31, 2018. https://hbr.org/2018/05/the-right-way-to-respond-to-negative-feedback.

Ibarra, Herminia. 2018. "The Authenticity Paradox." TEDx Video. June 27, 2018. 16:53. https://www.youtube.com/watch?v=CIjI3TmEzrs.

Lozoff, Bo. 1999. *Deep and Simple: A Spiritual Path for Modern Times.* Edited by Joshua Lozoff. Durham, NC: The Human Kindness Foundation.

Mate, Gabor. 2023. "Find Your True Self When You Feel Lost, Authenticity." Way of Thinking. January 22, 2023. 11:35. https://www.youtube.com/watch?v=WSAWp-nLysQ.

Morgan, Nick. 2008. "How to Become an Authentic Speaker." *Business Communication* (blog), *Harvard Business Review*. November 2008. https://hbr.org/2008/11/how-to-become-an-authentic-speaker.

Nevid, Jeffrey S., Spencer A. Rathus, and Beverly Greene. 2012. *Abnormal Psychology in a Changing World*. London, UK: Pearson.

Online Etymology Dictionary. 2023. "Authentic." Accessed June 2, 2023. https://www.etymonline.com/word/authentic.

Riutta, Shelley. 2021. "Authentic versus Conditioned Self." Holistic Business School.

Serlin, Emma. 2015. "Authentic Speech: What Does It Mean and Why Should You Care?" *Communication Tips* (blog), *London Speech Workshop*. July 23, 2015. https://blog.londonspeechworkshop.com/authentic-speech-care.

Sheldon, M. Kennon, Richard M. Ryan, Laird J. Rawsthorne, and Barbara Ilardi. 1997. "Trait Self and True Self: Cross-Role Variation in the Big-Five Personality Traits and Its Relations with Psychological Authenticity and Subjective Well-Being." *Journal of Personality and Social Psychology* 73, no. 6 (December): 1380-1393. https://psycnet.apa.org/doi/10.1037/0022-3514.73.6.1380.

Smerek, Ryan. 2021. "Can Being Authentic Improve Your Performance? Research on the Benefits and Limitations of Authenticity." *Authenticity* (blog), *Psychology Today*. October 6, 2021. https://www.psychologytoday.com/us/blog/learning-at-work/202110/can-being-authentic-improve-your-performance.

Tsaousides, Theo. 2017. "How to Conquer the Fear of Public Speaking. Are You Ready for a Standing Ovation?" *Fear* (blog), *Psychology Today*. November 28, 2017. https://www.psychologytoday.com/us/blog/smashing-the-brainblocks/201711/how-conquer-the-fear-public-speaking.

Wood, Alex Matthew, Alex P. Linley, John Maltby, Michael Baliousis, and Stephen Joseph. 2008. "The Authentic Personality: A Theoretical and Empirical Conceptualization and the Development of the Authenticity Scale." *Journal of Counseling Psychology* 55, no. 3. (July). https://psycnet.apa.org/doi/10.1037/0022-0167.55.3.385.

CONNECT AND COMMUNICATE IN A MAGNETIC STYLE

American Psychological Association. 2023. "Shyness." American Psychological Association. Accessed May 27, 2023. https://www.apa.org/topics/shyness.

Aron, Elaine N. 2016. *The Highly Sensitive Person: How to Thrive When the World Overwhelms You*. New York, NY: Harmony.

Beebe, Steven A., and Susan J. Beebe. 2010. *A Concise Public Speaking Handbook, Third Edition*. Boston, MA: Allyn & Bacon.

Dhillon, Navdeep, and Gurvinder Kaur. 2021. "Self-Assessment of Teachers' Communication Style and Its Impact on Their Communication Effectiveness: A Study of Indian Higher Educational Institutions." *SAGE Open* 11, no. 2. (June). https://doi.org/10.1177/21582440211023173.

Emerson, Mary Sharp. 2022. "Is Your Workplace Communication Style as Effective as It Could Be?" *Professional Development* (blog), Harvard Division of Continuing Education. February 4, 2022. https://professional.dce.harvard.edu/blog/is-your-workplace-communication-style-as-effective-as-it-could-be/.

Hamilton, Cheryl. 2011. *Communicating for Results: A Guide for Business and the Professions*, 9th ed. Boston, MA: Wadsworth Cengage Learning.

Houston, Elaine. 2019. "Introvert vs Extrovert: A Look at the Spectrum & Psychology." *Meaning and Values* (blog), *Positive Psychology*. March 27, 2023. https://positivepsychology.com/introversion-extroversion-spectrum/#definitions.

Noll Wilson, Sarah. 2022. *Don't Feed the Elephants: Overcoming the Art of Avoidance to Build Powerful Partnerships*. Austin, TX: Lioncrest.

Nordquist, Richard. 2019. "Feedback in Communication Studies: Glossary of Grammatical and Rhetorical Terms." ThoughtCo. July 3, 2019. https://www.thoughtco.com/feedback-communication-term-1690789.

Schaefer, Bill. 2015. "Mental Health Therapist Training." Handout. Des Moines, Iowa.

PASSION LEADS TO A MAGNETIC MESSAGE

Clifton, Don, and Tom Rath. 2017. *StrengthsFinder 2.0 From Gallup: Discover Your CliftonStrengths*. New York, NY: Gallup Press.

Duck, Steve, and David T. McMahan. 2009. *The Basics of Communication: A Relational Perspective*. Los Angeles, CA: Sage Publishing.

Forleo, Marie. 2015. "Elizabeth Gilbert Talks 'Big Magic:' Fear, Failure, & the Mystery of Creativity." Marie Forleo. September 22, 2015. 47:75. https://www.youtube.com/watch?v=HyUYa-BnjU8&t=71s.

Heath, Chip, and Dan Heath. 2008. *Made to Stick: Why Some Ideas Survive and Others Die*. UK: Arrow Books.

Keller, Gary, and Jay Papasan. 2012. *The One Thing: The Surprisingly Simple Truth Behind Extraordinary Results*. Austin, TX: Bard Press.

Lozoff, Bo. 1999. *Deep and Simple: A Spiritual Path for Modern Times*. Edited by Joshua Lozoff. Durham, NC: The Human Kindness Foundation.

Lucas, Stephen E. 2012. *The Art of Public Speaking*. New York, NY: McGraw-Hill.

Webster's New World Dictionary. 1988. Neufeldt, Victoria E. Editor in Chief. Third College Edition. New York, NY: Webster's New World Dictionaries a Division of Simon and Schuster, Inc.

Zarefsky, David. 2011. *Public Speaking: Strategies for Success*, 6th ed. Boston, MA: Allyn & Bacon.

THE WHO THAT WE SHARE: WE'RE ALL STORYTELLERS

Bhalla, Jag. 2013. "It Is in Our Nature to Need Stories." *Guest Blog* (blog), *Scientific American*. May 8, 2013. https://blogs.scientificamerican.com/guest-blog/it-is-in-our-nature-to-need-stories/.

Bakehouse, Tina. 2016. "Instead of Move On, Move Forward." Jude Treder-Wolff. May 16, 2016. 13:51. https://www.youtube.com/watch?v=755cP_VgNdg.

Bowles, Meg, Catherin Burns, Jenifer Hixson, Sarah Austin Jenness, and Kate Tellers. 2022. *How to Tell a Story: The Essential Guide to Memorable Storytelling from The Moth.* New York, NY: Crown.

Brewster, Annie. 2021. "Stories Connect Us." *Harvard Health Blog* (blog), Harvard University. July 21, 2021. https://www.health.harvard.edu/blog/stories-connect-us-202107212550.

Clark, Roy Peter. 2006. *Writing Tools: 55 Essential Strategies for Every Writer.* New York, NY: Little, Brown Spark.

Hutchens, David. 2015. *Circle of the 9 Muses: A Storytelling Field Guide for Innovators and Meaning Makers.* Hoboken, NJ: John Wiley & Sons, Inc.

King, Frank. 2017. "A Matter of Laugh or Death." TED Talks. March 6, 2017. 19:10. https://www.youtube.com/watch?v=aBUXND5BD4M&t=516s.

Sanni, Anthony. 2023. "Master Storytellers Think Differently - 3 Mindsets You Can Adopt to Improve Your Storytelling." *The Blog* (blog), *Anthony Sanni*. March 4, 2023. https://anthonysanni.com/blog/storytelling-storyteller-principles-mindsets.

Sinek, Simon. 2014. "How Great Leaders Inspire Action." TED. September 28, 2014. 17:47. https://www.ted.com/talks/simon_sinek_how_great_leaders_inspire_action/c?language=en.

Zak, Paul. 2014. "Why Your Brain Loves Good Storytelling" *Business Communication* (blog), *Harvard Business Review*. October 28, 2014. https://hbr.org/2014/10/why-your-brain-loves-good-storytelling.

PREPARE AN AUDIENCE-CENTERED MAGNETIC MESSAGE

Bolte Taylor, Jill. 2009. "My Stroke of Insight." TED Talks. March 13, 2009. 20:11. https://www.youtube.com/watch?v=UyyjU8fzEYU.

Clark, Roy Peter. 2006. *Writing Tools: 55 Essential Strategies for Every Writer.* New York, NY: Little, Brown Spark.

Duarte Inc. 2023. "The Duarte Method." Duarte. Accessed January 11, 2023. https://www.duarte.com/approach/duarte-method/.

Gates, Bill. 2015. "The Next Outbreak? We're Not Ready." TED Talks. April 3, 2015. 8:36. https://www.youtube.com/watch?v=6Af6b_wyiwI.

ISU Writing Center. 2016. "Concrete and Specific Language." Idaho State University. https://www.isu.edu/media/libraries/student-success/tutoring/handouts-writing/editing-and-mechanics/Concrete-and-Specific-Language.pdf.

Jobs, Steve. 2005. "Steve Jobs' 2005 Stanford Commencement Address." Stanford Video. June 12, 2005. 15:04. https://www.youtube.com/watch?v=UF8uR6Z6KLc.

Lucas, Stephen E. 2012. *The Art of Public Speaking*. New York, NY: McGraw-Hill.

Obama, Michelle. 2008. "Michelle Obama at the 2008 DNC." BarakObamaDotCom. August 25, 2008. 20:13. https://www.youtube.com/watch?v=sTFsBo9KhqI.

Robinson, Ken. 2007. "Do Schools Kill Creativity?" TED Talks. January 6, 2007. 20:03. https://www.youtube.com/watch?v=iG9CE55wbtY&t=38s.

Quercus. 2006. *The Greatest American Speeches: The Stories and Transcripts of the Words that Changed Our History*. London, UK: Quercus Publishing Ltd.

Zarefsky, David. 2011. *Public Speaking Strategies for Success*, 6th ed. London, UK: Pearson.

FOSTER CURIOSITY AND PLAYFUL CREATIVITY TO BE A MAGNETIC SPEAKER

Cameron, Julia. 2016. *The Artist's Way: A Spiritual Path to Higher Creativity*. New York, NY: Penguin Random House LLC.

Citron, Hollis. 2022. "Let's Chat About Protecting Audiences from Boring Speakers & Speeches." *Creative Conversations with Hollis Citron*. Released December 17, 2022. 1 hr. 2 min. https://muckrack.com/podcast/creative-conversations-with-hollis-citron/episodes/7314901-lets-chat-about-protecting-audiences-from-/.

Dewar, Gwen. 2023. "The Social and Cognitive Benefits of Play: Effects on the Learning Brain." *Parenting Science* (blog). Accessed July 7, 20123. https://parentingscience.com/benefits-of-play/.

Gilbert, Elizabeth. 2015. *Big Magic: Creative Living Beyond Fear*. New York, NY: Riverhead Books.

Jones, Richard H. 2018. *Mystery 101: An Introduction to the Big Questions and the Limits of Human Knowledge*. Albany, NY: SUNY Press.

Leslie, Ian. 2015. *Curious: The Desire to Know and Why Your Future Depends on it*. New York, NY: Basic Books.

Maxwell, John. 2017. "5 Tips to Spark Creativity in Others." *Global Leadership*. October 23, 2017. https://globalleadership.org/articles/leading-others/5-tips-spark-creativity-others-john-c-maxwell/?locale=en.

Quinn, Sara, Seamus Donnelly, and Evan Kidd. 2018. "The Relationship Between Symbolic Play and Language Acquisition: A Meta-Analytic Review." *Developmental Review* 49, (September 2018): 121-135. https://doi.org/10.1016/j.dr.2018.05.005.

FINDING THE FLOW IN PREPARATION AND PRESENTATION LEADS TO MAGNETIC SPEAKING

Berka, Chris, Adrienne Behneman, Natalie Kintz, and Robin Johnson. 2010. "Accelerating Training Using Interactive Neuro-Educational Technologies: Applications to Archery, Golf and Rifle Marksmanship." *The International Journal of Sport & Society* 1, (January). https://www.researchgate.net/publication/236159566_SPORT_SOCIETY_Accelerating_Training_Using_Interactive_Neuro-_Educational_Technologies_Applications_to_Archery_Golf_and_Rifle_Marksmanship.

Charnas, Dan. 2016. *Everything in Its Place: The Power of Mise-En-Place to Organize Your Life, Work, and Mind.* Emmaus, PA: Rodale Books.

Csikszentmihalyi, Mihaly. 1990. *Flow: The Psychology of Optimal Experience.* New York, NY: HarperPerennial Modern Classics.

Fischer, David B., Aaron D. Boes, Athena Demertzi, Henry C. Evrard, Steven Laureys, Brian L. Edlow, Hesheng Liu, Clifford B. Saper, Alvaro Pascual-Leone, Michael D. Fox, and Joel C. Geerling. 2016. "A Human Brain Network Derived from Coma-Causing Brainstem Lesions." *Neurology* 87, no. 23 (December 2016): 2427–2434. https://n.neurology.org/content/87/23/2427.

Newport, Cal. 2016. *Deep Work: Rules for Focused Success in a Distracted World.* New York, NY: Grand Central Publishing.

Zimmer, Sandra. n.d. "The Zimmer Method can Help You Hack the Flow State for Public Speaking." *Sandra Zimmer and the Self Expression Center Blog* (blog). Accessed March 21, 2023. https://www.sandrazimmer.com/the-zimmer-method-can-help-you-hack-the-flow-state-for-public-speaking/.

AM I PREPARED TO BE THE INSTRUMENT OF MY OWN MESSAGE?

DeMichele, Mary, and Scott Kuennke. 2021. "Short-Form, Comedy Improv Affects the Functional Connectivity in the Brain of Adolescents with Complex Developmental Trauma as Measured by qEEG: A Single Group Pilot Study." *NeuroRegulation* 8, no. 1 (March). https://doi.org/10.15540/nr.8.1.2.

Drinko, Clay. 2021. "New Research Highlights the Brain-Boosting Benefits of Improv: New Neuroscience Evidence Points to Improv as a Potential Trauma Treatment." *Confidence* (blog), *Psychology Today.* March 30, 2021. https://www.psychologytoday.com/us/blog/play-your-way-sane/202103/new-research-highlights-the-brain-boosting-benefits-improv.

Gesell, Izzy. 2015. "Yes and Facilitation." Applied Improvisation Conference Workshop. September 17, 2015. Montreal, Canada: Izzy Gesell.

Kulhan, Bob. 2017. *Getting to "Yes And": The Art of Business Improv.* Stanford, CA: Stanford University.

Quintanilla, Kelly M., and Shawn T. Wahl. 2014. *Business and Professional Communication: KEYS for Workplace Excellence. Second Edition*. Los Angeles, CA: Sage Publications.

Schwenke, Diana, Maja Dschemuchadse, Lisa Rasehorn, Dominik Klarhölter, and Stefan Scherbaum. 2020. "Improv to Improve: The Impact of Improvisational Theater on Creativity, Acceptance, and Psychological Well-Being." *Journal of Creativity in Mental Health* 16, no. 1 (January): 31-48. https://doi.org/10.1080/15401383.2020.1754987.

Shipon-Blum, Elisa. n.d. "What is Selective Mutism? Selective Mutism—A Comprehensive Overview." SMart Center: Selective Mutism, Anxiety, and Related Disorders Treatment Center. Accessed May 31, 2023. https://selectivemutismcenter.org/whatisselectivemutism.

Smart, James. 2021. "22 Great Improv Games for Better Collaboration (and Fun!)." *Session Lab Blog* (blog). November 10, 2021. https://www.sessionlab.com/blog/improv-games/.

Taylor, Lucy, and Tzuki Stewart. 2022. "Let Go, Notice More, Use Everything." *Why Play Works*. Released June 6, 2022. 56 min. 12 sec. https://whyplayworks.com/episode/let-go-use-more-notice-everything.

Treder-Wolff, Jude. 2023. "How Improv Can Flip Your Creativity 'Switch.'"

judetrederwolff (blog). June 5, 2023. https://judetrederwolff.medium.com/how-improv-can-flip-your-creativity-switch-95445e3e5f6f.

THE WHO THAT WE MOVE: POISE IS A VERB

Angelou, Maya. 1993. "Maya Angelou's Poem 'On the Pulse of Morning.'" Clintonlibrary42. January 20, 1993. 6:26. https://www.youtube.com/watch?v=59xGmHzxtZ4.

Brown, Brené. 2010. "The Power of Vulnerability." TED. December 23, 2010. 19:18. https://www.ted.com/talks/brene_brown_the_power_of_vulnerability/c.

Clear, James. n.d. "Atomic Habits Summary." Review of *Atomic Habits* by James Clear. Accessed May 31, 2023. https://jamesclear.com/atomic-habits-summary.

Cuddy, Amy. 2015. *Presence: Bringing Your Boldest Self to Your Biggest Challenges*. New York, NY: Hachette Book Company.

Fey, Tina. 2010. "Tina Fey Acceptance Speech: 2010 Mark Twain Prize." The Kennedy Center. October 21, 2010. 8:23. https://www.youtube.com/watch?v=M826uPUNCro.

Forbes, Thompson, and Shannon Evans. 2022. "From Anticipation to Confidence: A Descriptive Qualitative Study of New Graduate Nurse Communication with Physicians." *Journal of Nursing Management* 30, no. 6 (May): 2039-2045. https://onlinelibrary.wiley.com/doi/10.1111/jonm.13656.

Lamott, Anne. 2012. "12 Truths I Learned from Life and Writing." TED. April 24, 2012. 15:44.
https://www.ted.com/talks/anne_lamott_12_truths_i_learned_from_life_and_writing?language=en.

LeBorgne, Wendy. 2018. "Vocal Branding: How Your Voice Shapes Your Communication Image." TED Talks. May 22, 2018. 12:21.
https://www.youtube.com/watch?v=p_ylzGfHKOs.

Louis-Dreyfus, Julia. 2023. "Julia Gets Wise with Jane Fonda." *Wiser Than Me with Julia Louis-*

Dreyfus, Released April 11, 2023. 47 min. 22 sec.
https://lemonadamedia.com/show/wiser-than-me-with-julia-louis-dreyfus/.

Mariolle Shelton, Tiffany. 2021. "Segment Intending Abraham Hicks How to Segment Intend." *Tiffany* (blog). May 20, 2021.
https://www.tiffanyshelton.com/segment-intending-abraham-hicks-how-to-segment-intend/.

McAfee, Barbara. 2016. "Bringing Your Full Voice to Life." TED Talks. May 19, 2016. 19:07.
https://www.youtube.com/watch?v=Ze763kgrWGg.

Morgan, Nick. 2014. *Power Cues: The Subtle Science of Leading Groups, Persuading Others, and Maximizing Your Personal Impact.* Boston, MA: Harvard Business Review Press.

Oxford Dictionary. 2023. "Poise." Oxford Learner's Dictionary. Accessed June 24, 2023.
https://www.oxfordlearnersdictionaries.com/us/definition/english/poise_1.

MAGNETIC SPEAKERS FORGIVE OTHERS AND THEMSELVES

Berkley University of California. 2023. "What Is Forgiveness?" *Greater Good Magazine* (blog), Berkley University. Accessed February 1, 2023.
https://greatergood.berkeley.edu/topic/forgiveness/definition.

Breines Juliana G., Myriam V. Thoma Danielle Gianferante Luke Hanlin. Xuejie Chen, Nicolas Rohleder. 2014. "Self-Compassion as a Predictor of Interleukin-6 Response to Acute Psychosocial Stress." *Brain Behavior Immunity.* 37 (November):109-14.
https://www.sciencedirect.com/science/article/abs/pii/S0889159113005370?via%3Dihub.

Eger, Edith Eva. 2018. *The Choice: Embrace the Possible.* New York, NY: Scribner.

Eger, Edith Eva. 2022. "Forgiveness: A Gift I Give Myself." Soul Search.
https://yoursoulsearch.org/.

Forleo, Marie. 2015. "Elizabeth Gilbert Talks 'Big Magic'—Fear, Failure, & the Mystery of Creativity." Marie Forelo. September 22, 2015. 47:56.
https://www.youtube.com/watch?v=HyUYa-BnjU8&t=71s.

Harwood, Elena M., and Nancy L. Kocovski. 2017. "Self-Compassion Induction Reduces Anticipatory Anxiety Among Socially Anxious Students." *Mindfulness 8,* (April): 1544-1551.
https://doi.org/10.1007/s12671-017-0721-2.

Harvard Health Publishing. 2021. "The Power of Forgiveness: The REACH Method Teaches How to Overcome Lingering Bad Feelings Toward Someone Who Did You Wrong." *Mind & Mood* (blog), Harvard Medical School. February 12, 2021. https://www.health.harvard.edu/mind-and-mood/the-power-of-forgiveness.

Howes, Ryan. 2009. "Four Elements of Forgiveness: What Does It Take to Forgive?" *Forgiveness* (blog), *Psychology Today*. September 4, 2009. https://www.psychologytoday.com/us/blog/in-therapy/200909/four-elements-forgiveness.

Laurence, Emily. 2023. "Forgiveness; How to Forgive Yourself and Others." *Health/ Mind* (blog), *Forbes Health*. January 27, 2023. https://www.forbes.com/health/mind/ways-to-forgive-yourself-and-others/.

Long, Phoebe. 2017. "Can Self-Compassion Make You Better at Public Speaking?" *Mind & Body*. (blog), *Greater Good Magazine*. September 25, 2017. https://greatergood.berkeley.edu/article/item/can_self_compassion_make_you_better_at_public_speaking

Long, Phoebe, and Kristin D. Neff. 2018. "Self-Compassion is Associated with Reduced Self-Presentation Concerns and Increased Student Communication Behavior." *Educational Psychology* 67 (October): 223-231. https://doi.org/10.1016/j.lindif.2018.09.003.

Neff, Kristin. 2023. *Self-Compassion.* "Definition of Self-Compassion." *Self-compassion* (blog). 2023. https://self-compassion.org/the-three-elements-of-self-compassion-2/.

Weir, Kirsten. 2017. "Forgiveness Can Improve Mental and Physical Health." *American Psychology Association* 48, no. 1. (January): 30. https://www.apa.org/monitor/2017/01/ce-corner.

THE PRACTICE: DO THE WORK

Blount, Jeb. 2023. "The 3 Ps that Hold You Back from Prospecting." *Jeb Blount's Sales Gravy.* June 28, 2018. 00:35. https://www.youtube.com/watch?v=8OBkxtzTG4A.

Cameron, Julia. 2016. *The Artist's Way: A Spiritual Path to Higher Creativity.* New York, NY: Penguin Random House LLC.

Dwyer, Karen Kangas. 1998. *Conquer Your Speechfright: Learn How to Overcome the Nervousness of Public Speaking.* Fort Worth, TX: Harcourt Brace College Publishers.

Ebrahimi, Omid V., Stale Pallesen, Robin M. F. Kenter, and Tine Nordgreen. 2019. "Psychological Interventions for the Fear of Public Speaking: A Meta-Analysis." *Frontiers in Psychology* 10, (March): 488. https://doi.org/10.3389%2Ffpsyg.2019.00488.

Greene, Richard. 2014. "The 7 Secrets of the Greatest Speakers in History." TED Talks. November 5, 2014. 18:24. https://www.youtube.com/watch?v=ioa61wFaF8A&t=674s.

Jin-Young, Kim. 2015. "The Effect of Personality, Situational Factors, and Communication Apprehension on a Blended Communication Course." Division of General Studies, *Indian Journal of Science and Technology* 8, no. 1: 1-7. https://dx.doi.org/10.17485/ijst/2015/v8iS1/60760.

Kaufman, Scott Barry. 2014. "Practice Alone Does Not Make Perfect, Studies Find." *Beautiful Minds* (blog), *Scientific American*. July 15, 2014. https://blogs.scientificamerican.com/beautiful-minds/practice-alone-does-not-make-perfect-studies-find/.

Kottawatta, Hemantha. 2019. "Big Five Personality and Communication Styles." Conference paper for Economic and Social Development: Book of Proceedings by Varazdin. October 17-18, 2019. https://www.proquest.com/openview/56a9317de2927e749ac84de6ac2e0e95/1.pdf?pq-origsite=gscholar&cbl=2033472.

Lawrenz, Lori, and Saundra Montijo. 2022. "Public Speaking Anxiety: What Is It and Tips to Overcome It." *Psych Central* (blog), *Psych Central*. March 8, 2022. https://psychcentral.com/anxiety/public-speaking-anxiety

Noll Wilson, Sarah. 2022. *Don't Feed the Elephants: Overcoming the Art of Avoidance to Build Powerful Partnerships.* Austin, TX: Lioncrest Publications.

O'Hair, Dan, Rob Stewart, and Hannah Rubenstein. 2012. *A Speaker's Guidebook: Text and Reference Fifth Edition.* Boston, MA: Bedford/St.Martin's.

Parnell, Laurel. 2008. *Tapping In: A Step-by-Step Guide to Activating Your Healing Resources Through Bilateral Stimulation: Reduce Anxiety, Sleep Better, Overcome Trauma.* Boulder, CO: Sounds True.

Pressfield, Steven. 2002. *The War of Art: Break Through the Blocks and Win Your Inner Creative Battles.* New York: Black Irish Entertainment LLC.

Stewart, Craig O., John McConnell III., Lori A. Stallings, and Rod Roscoe. 2019. "Growth Mindset: Associations with Apprehension, Self-Perceived Competence, and Beliefs about Public Speaking." *Basic Communication Course Annual* 31, no. 6 (January): 44-63. https://www.researchgate.net/publication/333433281_Growth_Mindset_Associations_with_Apprehension_Self-Perceived_Competence_and_Beliefs_about_Public_Speaking.

Made in the USA
Monee, IL
19 November 2023

46798590R00154